Conversations

This book belongs to:

Jackie Ina Kane
20 Flesherin
Point
Isle of Lewis
DA86 OHE.

Conversations

by

JOHN HATCHER

Illustrated
by
Audrey Marcus
and
Brian Parsons

GEORGE RONALD
OXFORD

George Ronald, Publisher
46 High Street, Kidlington, Oxford, OX5 2DN

British Library Cataloguing in Publication Data

Hatcher, John
Conversations.
I. Title
813'.54 [J]

ISBN 0-85398-275-9 Pbk

Photoset by Action Typesetting Ltd., Gloucester
Printed and bound in the U.S.A. by The Maple Vail Book Manufacturing Group

For

Badí' 1853–1870, martyred age 17
Rúḥu'lláh 1884–1896, martyred age 12
Mona 1967–1983, martyred age 16

And all the Bahá'í youth who through the years have shown us
with their deeds a glimpse of the future words cannot adequately
portray

Every child is potentially the light of the world — and at the same time its darkness; wherefore must the question of education be accounted as of primary importance.   'Abdu'l-Bahá

CONTENTS

1

The Visitor

THOUGH they had come to this land as prisoners in 1868, the Persian Bahá'ís who dwelt in and around the Palestinian towns of 'Akká and Haifa had managed to win the hearts of both the local inhabitants and the Ottoman government agents, who were officially their wardens. After the passing of Bahá'u'lláh in 1892 at the mansion of Bahjí a few kilometres northeast of 'Akká, His son 'Abdu'l-Bahá had directed the small community as well as the administrative affairs of the Bahá'í Faith as a whole, which by the turn of the century had spread to Europe and America. With the inspired work of teachers such as Martha Root and Agnes Alexander, the religion was also gaining adherents throughout the rest of the world.

When 'Abdu'l-Bahá went on His lengthy three-year sojourn from the Holy Land in 1910 to visit the newly-formed communities in Europe and America, the believers were confirmed in their enthusiasm for what they believed to be a clear sign of renewal and hope amid the rumours of impending war. By the time 'Abdu'l-Bahá returned to Haifa in December of 1913, His health, already shattered by seventy years of unrelenting service and physical hardship, had deteriorated further. But He was eagerly welcomed back by the

Bahá'í community dwelling in the Holy Land which looked upon Him as the sole source of advice and assistance, and pilgrims streamed from East and West to see Him.

'Abdu'l-Bahá became increasingly concerned about how the believers would react when He died, something He expressed in a Tablet several months later when He said: 'The time is coming when I shall be no longer with you. I have done all that could be done. I have served the Cause of Bahá'u'lláh to the utmost of my ability. I have laboured night and day, all the years of my life. O, how I long to see the loved ones taking upon themselves the responsibilities of the Cause!'

As the tensions in Europe and Turkey mounted, it became obvious that pilgrims, especially those from the West, were no longer safe in this stronghold of the Ottoman Empire. On 28th June, 1914, Austrian Archduke Franz Ferdinand was assassinated. The war that 'Abdu'l-Bahá had predicted was imminent, and on 29th June, 1914, 'Abdu'l-Bahá instructed the Bahá'í pilgrims to leave 'Akká and Haifa. More and more 'Abdu'l-Bahá and the other Bahá'ís were cut off from the rest of the world so that by the autumn of 1914 when the Ottoman Empire declared a Holy War and aligned itself with Germany and Austria-Hungary, the Bahá'ís in this Ottoman territory were held in even closer scrutiny than before.

'Abdu'l-Bahá's own concerns were heightened still further by the machinations of Dr Fareed who, though one of 'Abdu'l-Bahá's companions on the journey to the West, had become a victim of his own greed. On the pretext of raising funds for the construction of a hospital on Mt Carmel, Dr Fareed had taken money from wealthy and well-meaning Bahá'ís like Phoebe Hearst and had greatly disturbed some of the newer converts to the Bahá'í Faith who were understandably shaken by such behaviour.

Amid this desperate confusion lived the Bahá'ís. In spite of the proximity of the war and their own precarious situation, 'Akká itself was thus far relatively untouched by the war. 'Abdu'l-Bahá assured the Bahá'ís they were safe, that the war would not come to the immediate vicinity, but the growing fear among the populace prompted

'Abdu'l-Bahá to direct the Bahá'ís living in 'Akká and Haifa to move to the safety of the countryside and the nearby Druze villages. Most were to go to the village of Abú-Sinán, a small settlement nestled in the foothills of Galilee, some ten kilometres east of 'Akká. 'Abdu'l-Bahá Himself was to remain behind in Haifa.

It was during the evacuation of the Bahá'ís from 'Akká in the autumn of 1914 that the family of Husayn and Nahid Mashhadi received an unexpected guest. Late one evening Nahid and her fourteen-year-old son Ali were packing valises with the clothes and household goods they would need. Ali's father, Husayn, was in Haifa getting instructions from 'Abdu'l-Bahá, and most of the other Bahá'ís had already left, including Ali's friend Neda and her family.

Ali had grown considerably during the past two years. He considered himself almost a man, though he was impatient to reach his fifteenth birthday when, according to Bahá'í law, he would attain the age of maturity. He was taller than most of the other boys his age, something he took pride in. So when there was a knock on the door, he told his mother he would answer it – he felt himself to be her protector in his father's absence during this perilous time.

When Ali opened the door, he was surprised to see standing there a dishevelled and weary traveller, a Persian man of about forty, and with him a young boy about Ali's age but smaller and slighter of build.

'Alláh-u-Abhá,' the man greeted Ali with a broad smile. The boy at his side simply looked down expressionless like a frightened stray dog. 'You must be Ali Mashhadi,' said the man. 'I am Sadiq-i-Yazdi. I am a cousin of yours. This is also your cousin, your first cousin Hasan Ali Yazdi.'

Ali welcomed the two into the small apartment just as Nahid entered the room. She immediately recognized Sadiq even though she had not seen him in over fifteen years – since she and Husayn had left Mashhad.

'Sadiq,' she said and embraced him. 'And is this your son? How in the world did you get here?'

'We have been travelling any way we could,' he said in a serious tone. 'Things are difficult in Persia even though our country is neutral. Instead of being an enemy to one side only, we are a battle-field for all.'

'And Khanum, how is Khanum? Sturdy as ever, I imagine?'

There was a poignant silence. Something was wrong. 'Your mother died six months ago,' said Sadiq. 'Because of the war, we were unable to send you word.'

Nahid bowed her head. There were no tears at first, only the stunned silence. It was one thing to lose one's parents after seeing them deteriorate over the years or after a severe and agonizing illness. Death may be expected then. It might even be accepted as a welcome release from suffering. But Nahid had not seen or heard from her mother in many years, for even though her mother had consented to Nahid's marriage to Husayn, she had never accepted the conversion of her daughters Nahid and Faezeh to the Bahá'í Faith. She was not fanatic in her beliefs as a Muslim – she did not consider them infidels; she simply did not understand why they had to break with their own inherited traditions and beliefs.

'She never did understand why Faezeh and I became Bahá'ís, did she?' asked Nahid weakly, holding back the flood of emotion as best she could.

'No,' said Sadiq sombrely, 'she never seemed to understand.'

Sadiq's confirmation touched Nahid to the heart and uncontrol-lably her breast heaved with sobs. She covered her face with her hands and left the room. Ali had never met his grandmother and so could hardly feel the impact of her passing, but he did feel the weight of his mother's grief.

In a few minutes Nahid returned to the room, calmer, her eyes red but a smile of resignation on her face. 'Forgive me,' she said to the frail boy who seemed dumbstruck by the strange surroundings and sudden outpouring of emotions.

'Nahid,' said Sadiq with his hand on the young boy's shoulder, 'this is your nephew Hasan, Faezeh's boy.'

Nahid was stunned. 'My child!' she said with more tears. 'My dear child, how wonderful to see you at last!' She took his hands and tried to see in his downcast face the image of her beloved sister who, together with her husband, had been killed in Yazd for their refusal to renounce their beliefs as Bahá'ís. 'Yes,' she said, tilting his chin with her fingers so that he looked into the kind and caring eyes of his aunt. 'Yes, I see her in your eyes and in your mouth, blended sweetly with your father's strength.'

Hasan brightened a little. He had been more distraught than anyone over his grandmother's death. She had raised him since he was three years old. Now, suddenly, he had been orphaned again, then taken by his Uncle Sadiq on the exhausting journey — some two thousand kilometres, much of it on foot, and much of that through the mountains.

The boy was obviously uncomfortable in this strange land among people he did not know, even though they were the closest kin he had. Nahid gently embraced him, then said to Ali, 'Take your cousin to the kitchen instantly and give him some teacakes.' Ali showed Hasan to the kitchen and tried as best he could to strike up a conversation, but the shy younger boy would only answer in brief monosyllables.

In the parlour Nahid asked Sadiq for more details about how her mother had died. She was pleased to learn that the Bahá'ís had helped at the funeral and that Fatimih had died peacefully in her sleep. Nahid still ached from the deep sorrow caused by her mother's rejection, but as Sadiq described Fatimih's last days, Nahid was filled with hope that her mother was now at peace and perhaps able to understand the truth that had so attracted her two daughters.

'But you must be utterly exhausted,' said Nahid.

'I am fine,' said Sadiq. 'It is such a bounty to see you that I can forget my aching feet. But why are you packing? Are you moving from 'Akká?'

'We are leaving in two days for Abú-Sinán, a Druze village just a short way from here. You must go with us.'

'I cannot,' said Sadiq. 'Tomorrow I must return to Isfáhán,' he said. 'With the war coming, I cannot afford to become trapped here — I must return to my own family. They need me now more than ever.'

'I don't understand,' said Nahid, 'what brought you all this distance?'

'Two things,' said Sadiq with a grin. 'First, I came to bring contributions to 'Abdu'l-Bahá from the Bahá'ís in Iṣfáhán.'

'And the second, might that have something to do with Hasan?'

Sadiq smiled. 'Well, can he stay with you?'

'Did you doubt for a minute that I would agree?' said Nahid with a benign look that reassured Sadiq the boy would be in the best of hands.

'No,' said Sadiq. 'Do you think I would have come all this way if I had any doubt? But let me caution you, he is a troubled youth.'

'Because of Mother's death?'

'Because of many things. I think he still harbours much pain from the death of Faezeh and Mihdi, even though he was only three years old when it happened. I think that's why he is so nervous now – being brought to live with a family who belong to the very religion that was indirectly responsible for the death of his mother and father.'

'What a shame that he knows so little about the beliefs for which his own parents gave their lives,' said Nahid.

'I'm afraid that was Fatimih's doing – I suspect she blamed the Bahá'í Faith for Faezeh's death, even though she must have known that it was misguided Muslims that killed her. But you knew her better than I.'

'Not for a long time, Sadiq. You were there in Yazd. You saw her. She rarely corresponded with me or answered my letters after Faezeh's death.'

'Well, in any case, young Hasan has inherited your mother's fears, I suspect.'

'He seems quite frail.'

'He needs many things. He needs to be outside more and, most of all, he needs to be with a family.'

'Faezeh's boy,' sighed Nahid. 'It's hard to believe.' Nahid and her sister had been very close. They had learned about the Bahá'í Faith together, had become Bahá'ís at the same time. And yet at the time of Faezeh's death, Nahid was too far away to attend the funeral. In fact she had not even received word of her sister's death until weeks later. And even though she grieved for months afterward, the event still felt incomplete to her, as if she had not really said farewell. She had never even had the chance to visit Faezeh's grave. But now, now with Faezeh's boy in her care, Nahid could contribute something to her sister's eternal peace of mind.

For the next several weeks life was hectic. After Sadiq returned to Persia to be with his own family, Hasan and the Mashhadis moved to Abú-Sinán where life was quite different from life in the city of 'Akká. The Druze themselves had long ago acquired great respect for the Bahá'ís, partly because Bahá'u'lláh Himself had visited the Druze villages in 1880. But the Druze had also come to respect and admire the personage of 'Abdu'l-Bahá, as well as the tolerance and kindness of the Bahá'ís themselves.

For example, a Bahá'í doctor, Dr Mu'ayyad, ran a small clinic at Abú-Sinán. Those who could afford it paid according to their means; the rest he treated for free. The Druze villagers were much impressed by this genuine demonstration of humanity.

The Bahá'ís also established a school next to the clinic where children were taught by Badí' Bushrú'í, a graduate of the Syrian Protestant College in Beirut, the same college that 'Abdu'l-Bahá's grandson Shoghi Effendi was starting to attend this same year.

Ali and Hasan attended classes at this school and in their spare time helped with chores or explored the countryside. It was exactly what Hasan needed, this life in the beautiful hills of Galilee. Soon he lost his ashen pallor – his cheeks became red from the briskly cold breezes which constantly swept the hills of Galilee in the winter, and his eyes became clearer and brighter.

Life was not easy. The Persian families were taken into the homes of the villagers so that Ali and Hasan shared a room with two other boys of a family that had originally come from the city of Tabríz. The food was simple fare: lentils and other dried beans, occasionally some goat's meat, milk or eggs. Of course there were always delicious olives from nearby trees, and Nahid, who assisted in the cooking, always managed to make even the most meagre victuals taste like a meal fit for an emperor.

The village chief, Shaykh Ṣáliḥ, offered his own house to 'Abdu'l-Bahá, but the Master, as 'Abdu'l-Bahá was titled by His father, chose to remain in Haifa where, in spite of His age, He tended to the needs of the local inhabitants who looked to 'Abdu'l-Bahá not only for spiritual advice but for every sort of assistance.

He did not disappoint them in this difficult time when food was growing ever more scarce because of the war. A good many of the local Templars and Turks in and around Haifa had been conscripted for the war by the Ottoman government, and the women and children were left to get along as best they could.

Because the Bahá'ís were Persians and Persia was neutral in the war, the Bahá'í men, like the Druze, were exempt from being compelled to fight. Therefore, 'Abdu'l-Bahá directed the Bahá'ís living on the rich farmlands in Galilee, particularly in 'Adasíyyih, to redouble their efforts in producing wheat to feed the bereft people in 'Akká and Haifa. On occasion, 'Abdu'l-Bahá Himself visited these villages to encourage the farm workers to do the best they could to serve the needs of the citizens.

The Bahá'í community was more isolated than ever, cut off as it was from almost all communication from the world outside the Holy Land. But for Hasan the war seemed a remote reality and the family life he had with the Mashhadis was something more pleasant than anything he had experienced before. He remained shy and wary of human association. He said little and nearly always looked down when in the presence of an adult or an unfamiliar child, but inside he began to feel a happiness totally new to him. Nahid and Husayn frequently commented to each other that their foster child seemed to be getting stronger, more relaxed.

'Don't set your hopes too high,' Husayn cautioned his wife one evening as they were walking on the outskirts of the village before dark. 'Remember, he has had over ten years of a life quite different from that of a Bahá'í family. God only knows what scars he bears deep within from the deaths of Faezeh and Mihdi.'

'I think he was too young to remember any of that,' said Nahid. 'After all, he was only three years old at the time.'

Husayn took his wife's hand. 'I remember some things quite clearly from when I was *two* years old, and that was *quite* some time ago.'

'So do I, now that you mention it, so do I.'

In February Ali's grandfather Moayyed was directed to go to 'Adasíyyih to help the Bahá'í villagers prepare for early spring planting. Moayyed had grown up on a farm in Mashhad and knew a great deal about how to increase the yield of crops. When Ali overheard Husayn telling Nahid that Grandfather was going to 'Adasíyyih, he asked if he and Hasan might go along.

'But Badí' Bushrú'í is such a fine teacher,' said Nahid. 'What will you two boys do about school?'

'Grandfather is a good teacher,' said Ali, 'and there is Maryam!' Ali had been to the Sea of Galilee and 'Adasíyyih once before as an eight-year-old boy, and he still vividly remembered the antics of Maryam, a Bahá'í teacher notorious for her sometimes outrageous methods of instructing children.

'Maryam is a fine teacher, Ali, but her classes are for little ones, not young men your age.' She used the term 'young men' to tantalize the boys with her regard for their maturity, hoping they might not go — the uncertainty of the war was what really concerned her. When nothing else seemed to persuade them, she said, 'Ali, what about the Arabs who raid those small villages?'

'It is safer there than it is here near the coast,' said Ali, 'and the Arabs no longer bother the village.'

'The boy is right,' said Husayn to his surprised wife — usually Husayn was the one to refuse the boy and she would end up having to soften his resolve on behalf of her adventurous son.

'What about you, Hasan?' she said. 'Do you really want to go, or would you rather stay here?' She was hoping he would stay and convince Ali to stay as well.

'Ali has told me about the beautiful waters of the Sea of Galilee,' said Hasan, 'how the mountains rise up all around it, and about the waterfalls on the Yarmuk River above 'Adasíyyih. I would dearly love to go with them!'

'I give up,' she said. 'I am outnumbered three to one — what chance do I have?'

2

Whispers in the Dark

I T WAS several days later that the boys left with Moayyed on the journey to 'Adasíyyih. They travelled in a wagon pulled by a single horse over a road that wound through the verdant hills of Galilee, the two boys perched on either side of the majestic elder who explained to them something of the history of this land as they rode.

Years before when Ali had gone to 'Adasíyyih, his family had left from Haifa following the road to Nazareth and on to Tiberias. The road from Abú-Sinán was more difficult, bumpy and steeper, but it was quite lovely, following the Na'amán River for a while, then crossing the beautiful farmlands and villages, finally winding its way down alongside the streams which emptied into the Sea of Galilee — Lake Tiberias as the local people called it.

Hasan had crossed over many mountains on his trip from Yazd to 'Akká. He had seen a variety of landscapes and rivers, but the rich pastureland and rolling hills of Galilee were totally different from the parched desert region around Yazd where he had grown up. It was like returning home, coming to this land so rich in history, so dear to the hearts of religious people throughout the world.

Both boys were content to watch the scenery as the wagon made its way up roads that anywhere else would not be called roads at all. They would pass by shepherds tending flocks of sheep, and wildflowers beside the roadway, yellow mostly, but with flecks of purple and red. And as they travelled, Moayyed talked about this land, about its rich heritage hundreds, even thousands of years before. He told them stories of the nation of Israel in the old days, and he talked about the many important events in the life of Christ that had occurred in this region.

By midday they reached the height of the hills overlooking the Sea of Galilee. When they reached the crest of the mountain ridge, the boys got their first glimpse of the exquisite blue water of the lake nestled in the valley below them surrounded by what seemed to be an endless vista of mountains. So startling was the beauty of this landscape that both boys made an audible gasp.

'Over there on the other side of the lake is the Golan,' said Moayyed. 'That way is Nazareth,' Moayyed continued, pointing in a southerly direction, 'and Haifa is beyond that.'

They stayed at this spot for about an hour as they ate the bread, cheeses and fruit that Nahid had prepared for them. Reluctantly they left this breathtaking view and proceeded on their way down toward the lake.

Several hours later they arrived at the village of Tiberias, and the boys asked Moayyed's permission to walk along the shore to watch the fishermen. There were a good many boats out, the men casting nets as they had done on these same waters for hundreds of years. The boys looked out across the expanse of blue water of the Sea of Galilee, a large oval about ten kilometres across from where they stood and about twenty kilometres long.

'Is it a lake or a sea?' asked Hasan.

'A large lake or a small sea,' said Ali with a smile. 'It has fresh water, but the hot springs in town and across the lake empty a lot of salt water into it. A long time ago, two thousand years ago during the time of Christ, it was called the Sea of Galilee or the Sea of Tiberias. Sometimes it is called Lake Kinneret, but I like to think of it as the Sea of Galilee because of the stories I have read in the Bible − about Christ when he first met his disciples here, or about the feeding of the five thousand people on the shore.'

'I'm not familiar with those stories,' said Hasan.

'But don't Muslims believe in Christ?' asked Ali, a little surprised.

'Oh, certainly. We believe in all the Prophets. In fact, Muḥammad talks about Christ in the Qur'án. But I have not read the Bible.'

'Oh,' said Ali. 'We'll have to get Moayyed to tell us some of the stories while we're here.'

'I would like that,' said Hasan with genuine interest.

'Yes,' said Ali. 'Moayyed says that the reason why this is called the Holy Land is because so much religious history occurred around here. In fact, the coming of Bahá'u'lláh to this land fulfilled ancient prophecies.' Ali went on to explain to Hasan what he had learned from various Bahá'í teachers regarding the rich history of the Holy Land, the prophecy in Hosea about the valley of 'Akká being a 'door of hope', the Islamic ḥadíth regarding the bounty of visiting the visitor of 'Akká.

Meanwhile Moayyed got a room for the three at the Grossmann Hotel, a large building constructed by the Templar community and sometimes called Das Deutsche or the German Hotel. 'Abdu'l-Bahá occasionally stayed there when he visited the Bahá'í properties in the Jordan River valley, and because it was the middle of the winter when few guests were visiting the lake or the baths, Moayyed managed to get the same room that 'Abdu'l-Bahá had used. It was a third-storey room which had a covered balcony looking out over the lake.

Before dinner Moayyed walked with the boys in the quietude of twilight on a narrow path above the town. They stopped at a grassy plot as Moayyed chanted an evening prayer, his aged voice rising and falling in melodious tones, casting the words of Bahá'u'lláh to the breezes of this ancient spot.

Hasan stood reverently, though he watched the face of Moayyed more than he listened to the words. The young boy was alone in a strange land, such a great distance from anyone or anything he knew, and yet here was this old man chanting unfamiliar words and Hasan felt somehow comforted. He was a meagre-looking lad, standing there in his frock coat and taj, his shoulders stooped, his frame thin, gaunt. He scrutinized the face of Moayyed and saw sincerity there.

The words were not intoned mechanically as one might recall memorized verses of scripture, and Hasan could tell from that clear face that those words possessed power for Ali's grandfather, that they came from his heart.

When he was finished, Moayyed uncrossed his arms and pointed directly across the lake. 'Over there are the farmlands where Bahá'u'lláh's brother Mírzá Muḥammad-Qulí lived. His family still works that land today. Then down at the southern end of the lake, that's where we will go tomorrow.' He pointed to his right where the Golan trailed off into the rich, fertile farmlands of the Jordan valley.

'The Yarmuk River flows from those hills across the lake and joins with the Jordan River. And on the other side of the Yarmuk is the village of 'Adasíyyih. Nearly thirty or more Bahá'í families live there. In fact, there are probably more Bahá'ís than anything else. We have an Ḥaẓíratu'l-Quds and some of the richest farms and best crops you will ever see.'

Both boys became excited about visiting the village, but Ali also longed to go out in one of the boats on the lake. 'Do Bahá'ís own any of the fish in this lake?' he asked with a smile.

'Only if you can catch them,' said Moayyed, 'only if you catch them.'

After a delicious meal of fish caught fresh that very day, the three retired early after their tiring carriage ride from Abú-Sinán. Before going to bed they opened the door to the balcony and went out to see the full moon rising from behind the Golan reflecting brightly in the water. A steady breeze blew in from across the lake, but even though it was winter, the air this evening was not terribly cold. They talked for awhile about the day's journey, then Ali chanted an evening prayer, softly so as not to disturb any of the other hotel guests.

Soon they were ready for bed, and within a few minutes after lying down all three were soundly asleep. Ali and Hasan were together in a bed on one side of the room, and Moayyed by himself in a smaller bed on the other. The beds were much more luxurious than the hard pallets they had become used to in the Druze village for the past weeks.

But in the middle of the night − what time he knew not − Moayyed was gradually wakened by the murmur of a muffled cry or moan − he could not tell which.

The noise was not loud and sounded as if it were coming from a great distance. After several minutes Moayyed was completely awake and tried to discover the source of the noise. As he sat up carefully, trying not to let his old creaking bones waken the boys, he realized that the sound was coming from Hasan.

The moon cast a beam of light on the floor so that Moayyed could see the young boy quite well. He considered whether he should do anything or simply allow sleep to take care of things. But when the moans became a little louder, Moayyed decided he should do something lest Hasan waken Ali. Nahid had cautioned Moayyed that Hasan often slept noisily and sometimes woke in the middle of the night with a gasp or a muted cry, but she had never talked with Hasan about it for fear it would embarrass the youth.

Moayyed slowly made his way to the bed, placed his hand gently on Hasan's shoulder and jostled him awake. When Hasan's eyes opened he had a startled and frightened look on his face. Then he saw Moayyed, a finger to his lips whispering, 'Shhhh. Try not to wake Ali.' Moayyed stood and motioned for Hasan to follow him to the balcony. There they sat down in white rattan chairs, and Moayyed gently closed the door half-way. Hasan rubbed his eyes, then looked down in embarrassment.

'Bad dreams?' asked Moayyed with the kindest voice he could muster.

'Yes, sir,' said Hasan, barely audible, his dark hair hanging across his forehead.

'Is it your grandmother's death that is causing these bad dreams?' Moayyed asked with a candour that surprised Hasan even though he found it reassuring.

'My parents,' said Hasan softly. 'Ever since Grandmother's death, I have started dreaming about them again.'

'The same dream?'

'More or less. I never see them in my dream. I was only three when it happened. All I remember about that night are voices and a lot of commotion. I remember I woke up, I called out for Mother, then I went back to sleep. I never saw them again.'

'And what happens in your dream?'

'The dream is set in different places, but always the same thing happens.' He looked out at the water reflecting the moonlight so tranquilly. 'Just now I dreamed I was at a large wooden boat dock at night. It was foggy, very foggy. It always is. I heard them being taken away and I called out, and I began running toward the sound of their voices. They called to me, and I could see the outline of their bodies at the railing of a boat, but the voices were confusing, as if they were calling through a whirlwind. I ran toward the boat as fast as I could, but the boat pulled away from the dock into the fog and disappeared before I could see their faces.'

Hasan's eyes were moist. He had never told anyone about these dreams, not even his grandmother. She had known — she had heard him in the night, but she felt she knew what he was suffering and the subject was too hard for her to deal with, so she never mentioned it.

Moayyed moved closer to the frightened boy and said nothing for a few minutes. Then he asked, 'What do you feel about these dreams? As you told me about them just now, what did you feel?'

Hasan thought. 'Sad,' he mumbled, 'sad and . . . and angry.'

'Angry? Angry at whom? Angry about what?'

'I don't know,' he said. Then he blurted out, 'Why did they have to be Bahá'ís?'

Moayyed knew then that the boy was angry at the Bahá'í Faith, perhaps because Hasan had learned they could have escaped death had they merely recanted, renounced their belief in Bahá'u'lláh. But they had chosen death instead. They had chosen to leave their son rather than change their beliefs — no, rather than even *say* they would change their beliefs. That simple lie was all that separated Hasan from his mother and father. Who could have begrudged them that?'

'Tell me, son. Do you think your parents regret their decision?'

'What?'

'Do you think your parents are disappointed that they decided to become Bahá'ís or that they are sorry they decided to give up their lives rather than deny their beliefs? Do you think they would want to change how they lived their lives?'

'They're dead,' Hasan said, as if that bare fact ended any speculation about what they might or might not think were they alive and able to think.

Moayyed leaned back, his aged eyes studying the young soul that sat before him, so maimed yet so full of possibilities. On his breath was a prayer for guidance and in his heart was such empathy and love that the boy surely must have sensed that the heart of this patriarch was a source of refuge.

Moayyed looked out across the lake, then pointed wordlessly at the full moon, now changed from gold to yellow to white as it rose like the morning sun up over the lake and all the hills of this ancient land, which the moon knew so intimately. 'Where does that light come from, Hasan.'

'What? The moonlight? What do you mean?'

'Where does it really come from?' Hasan was snatched from his sad thoughts to ponder the enigmatic question.

'What is the source of moonlight?'

'Why, the sun.'

'Yes. The light of the sun shines on the moon and what we see is but a reflection of that light, correct?'

'Yes,' said Hasan, a bit perplexed.

'Then the moon has no light of its own?'

'I guess not, no. I mean the light it has is its own in a way. It shares that light with us.'

'But the source of its light is not from within itself. Its light comes from another source, from the sun?'

'Yes.'

'And yet you cannot see that source right now, can you?'

'Not right now I can't. But I saw it today. I will see it tomorrow.'

'But what if you had not seen the sun before. What if you were a prisoner and were only let outside at night-time. Would you still believe the moon had no light of its own or that the source of its light was something else?'

'I don't know.' Hasan tried to imagine himself in such a circumstance, a perpetual prisoner always hidden from the sun, in a cave, perhaps, or in a house without windows. 'I suppose not,' he concluded, 'not unless someone explained it to me and showed me how it worked. They could show me a model, explain how the earth rotates so that the sun is no longer visible. I think if someone showed me a picture and explained it clearly, I might believe.'

'Very well, then answer this. When the moon sets and that reflected light is no longer visible, has the sunlight vanished as well?'

'Of course not,' said Hasan with a smile, now becoming amused at the old man's puzzles. 'Of course not.'

'Hasan, it is the same with the relationship between our bodies and our souls. In this life our bodies are instruments that our souls play, and the life we live here is like music ... yes, very much like music.'

'What do you mean?'

'When you hear someone play a santúr, the wood strikes the strings and beautiful melodies are let loose in the air. Is the music within the santúr itself?'

'Yes,' said Hasan, then he added thoughtfully, 'well, not exactly. The sound comes from the santúr, but the music, the melody, that is in the mind of the musician.'

'Then the santúr is important because it lets us know the mind and heart of the artist, but it is not responsible for the composition?'

'Yes, that's right.'

'Then without the santúr the composition might still exist?'

'How do you mean?'

'In the heart and mind of the musician, the tune might still exist.'

'Yes, I suppose so.'

'And the santúr is simply an instrument, a mirror that allows the artist to show us what is in his heart?'

'Yes, that's true,' said Hasan, suddenly intrigued by the thought.

'And when the santúr can no longer be played, when the strings break or the wood decays or becomes warped, or perhaps the instrument is simply badly out of tune, does that mean the music no longer exists?'

'No,' Hasan admitted.

'It is the same way with our bodies and our souls, my son,' said Moayyed, taking the boy's hand briefly to make his point. 'Our bodies are instruments for the soul, mirrors reflecting us to the world. They are like actors or mimes giving voice and movement and form to our thoughts and feelings.'

'I see what you mean,' said Hasan.

'And sometimes the body is no longer an apt instrument of the soul's music. Take me, for example. I am an old man, my body can hardly keep up with what I wish to express, yet in my soul I still may contrive all sorts of exotic and lovely tunes. And it is the same with young people as well. If you were suddenly deprived of movement — God forbid — if you were suddenly paralyzed, could you still learn?'

'Yes,' said Hasan, 'of course I could.'

'And you could still be a good person or a bad person, a kind person or a wicked person.'

'Yes, I guess — in my mind I could still have good and bad thoughts.'

'And you could harbour revenge and hatred or love and kindliness, even though no one would know, because the instrument of your soul would be unable to convey what is happening in your soul to those around you, correct?'

'Yes, I agree.'

'Now, look at the moon. When it is gone from the sky, we can no longer enjoy the reflection of the sun's beauty in the night sky, but you will not question whether the sun still exists, will you?'

'No,' said Hasan with a smile. 'Of course I won't.'

'Hasan,' said Moayyed, taking the boy's hand again, 'your parents are no longer visible to you, but the light that shone so beautifully through them in this physical life is still apparent in the next world.'

'You mean right now my mother and father are thinking and talking? They know about me?'

'Yes, I am sure of it. You know, Bahá'u'lláh asks in one Tablet how can we imagine that the Prophets would have allowed themselves to be so mistreated if they were not sure that there was a life beyond this life. He said, ''How could such Souls have consented to surrender themselves unto their enemies if they believed all the worlds of God to have been reduced to this earthly life?'''

'But how can you be sure?' said Hasan, somewhat comforted by Moayyed's observations, but still wanting a certitude, a conviction which would turn his doubts into ease of heart.

'Hasan, is birth something good or something forbidding and horrible?'

'It is very good,' he answered.

'Why is that?'

'Because it is a beginning. Because a child is pure and innocent. The child is full of possibilities and the family is full of hope.'

'But what if you were about to be born? What if you were in the womb of your mother? What if ...,' Moayyed paused, trying to contrive an appropriate analogy. 'What if you were one of three triplets — yes, there is you and Saba and Hormoz. You are all about to be born, but, of course, you can only be born one at a time.' Hasan laughed softly so as not to disturb Ali.

'Now, you have lived together your whole lives, nine whole months. You have watched each other grow and change and have come to love each other very much. Then suddenly, just when everything seems comfortable and nice, you and Hormoz see Saba disappear from sight! My goodness, what do you think has happened?'

'He has been born?'

'Ah, but you do not know that because no one has been able to tell you what birth is. All the two of you know is that he has disappeared. Are you not concerned?'

'Yes,' said Hasan more seriously. 'I see what you mean. Yes, I guess we might wonder what had happened to Saba.'

'Might you not say that he had died, that he had ceased to be?'

'Perhaps.'

'Of course you would. And you and Hormoz would miss him terribly. What is more, you would wonder if the same thing was going to happen to you! But what if we could communicate with you? What could we tell you to assure you that everything is all right, that Saba is fine?'

'You could tell me that when I enter this world I will be able to run and play and go in Ali's sailboat. You could explain how beautiful it is to see the moon shining over the Sea of Galilee.'

'But would you believe it?'

'I might.'

'And would you begin to understand that what you had thought of as death was really a beginning, a process of being born into another world full of possibilities, full of hope, a world where you could finally make use of those arms and legs and eyes and ears you had been developing for nine long months.'

'I'm not sure,' said Hasan. 'I think I would have to learn to trust you first before I would believe it.'

'Don't just take our word for it. Think logically. If there was no life but the life in the womb, then why did you need to develop arms and legs and senses, all the tools for this life?'

'True.'

'And if the purpose of this life is simply to do physical things, then why do our bodies stop developing when we are barely twenty years of age, the very time we are really only beginning to develop our minds and our knowledge of life?'

'I don't know.'

'And why is it we are supposed to become wiser and better as we grow older? What are we preparing for? Does it make sense that we are preparing our minds and souls for obliteration?'

'I guess that really wouldn't make sense, would it?'

'Hasan, a passage in *The Hidden Words* states: "I have made death a messenger of joy to thee. Wherefore dost thou grieve?" It's the same sort of thing we might say to the three of you there in your mother's womb. Don't be afraid of birth. What you think is death is only an entrance into a vaster and more perfect life.'

'And you believe that's where my parents are now?'

'I am certain of it.'

Hasan smiled. It was not a large smile. He looked up into the night sky. Not many stars could be seen because the moon was so bright that it was hard to look at. He was not absolutely sure of what lay ahead for him or where his parents were, but he did feel better inside.

He looked at Moayyed, Moayyed with the scars of age, Moayyed whose eyes seemed as if they must always have looked that way, as if they had never been young. 'I still miss them,' said Hasan.

'That never changes,' said Moayyed. 'I still miss my own father, I who am a grandfather and a great-grandfather still miss my father. But I don't worry about him, you see? I long for him, I would dearly love to see him, to hear his words, to hear his laughter, to touch his face, but I know he is taken care of and may be taking care of me. Furthermore, I know before too long I will see him again.'

Hasan thought for a moment, then looked at Moayyed's eyes. The conviction in those eyes momentarily melted away Hasan's fears. He stood up and stretched his arms. 'I am ready to sleep now,' he said.

The two moved back into the room, two dark shadows silhouetted on the floor by the moon's radiance, one old and bent, bearded, the other thin and fragile. Moayyed helped Hasan slip under the covers, then, as Moayyed was about to turn to go to his own bed, Hasan tugged on the old man's sleeve.

'Thank you,' he whispered. Moayyed patted his shoulder and went back to his own bed. He slowly crawled under the covers then lay there thinking about his own father and mother. He wondered about time in the next world. How far along were they now, now that so much time had passed since they had been born into that world. What did they know? What marvels could they show him now, what music of the soul?

3

The City of Certitude

THE night-time conversation with Moayyed had comforted Hasan – he had slept 'the sleep of the little angels', as his grandmother called it. But one talk, however comforting and reassuring for the moment, could hardly alleviate all the doubts and fears that had over the years festered within him like an untended wound. His grandmother had been a conscientious guardian, but she herself had been confused, not believing in the Bahá'í Faith and yet not knowing what to feel about her own beliefs as a Muslim. After all, it had been the mullas who had been directly responsible for inciting the townspeople against the Bahá'ís. It was they who bore the guilt for the death of her daughter and son-in-law.

As a result of these confused feelings, Fatimih had raised Hasan cautiously with regard to matters of religion. She was not disdainful of the Bahá'í Faith, but neither did she permit him to associate with the other Bahá'ís in Yazd or to attend Bahá'í classes. She taught him to pray and read the Qur'án. He thought of himself as a Muslim, and yet he knew why his parents had been martyred, and he himself was sometimes shunned and ridiculed at school and in the streets by other children because his parents had been Bahá'ís.

The end result of such an ambivalent upbringing upon this remarkably perceptive and intelligent young boy was now apparent. He was quiet, solemn, retiring. He rarely participated in physical games or sports, though he had become fascinated with the idea of fishing, something totally alien to his own desert village of Yazd. Insofar as his religious beliefs were concerned, he merely went through the motions. He prayed and sometimes sensed a Presence listening to those prayers and aware of his dilemma. But the only time he had felt sure of his belief in God occurred when he was by himself on the rooftop of his grandmother's house watching the stars on a summer night. He often recalled that evening when he looked into the night sky and mysteriously felt comforted, as if by an unseen physician.

He thought very little of his grandmother's beliefs. They seemed more akin to children's stories than any sort of reality he could imagine, especially her frequent allusion to Paradise as a physical place of angels and djinn. So when she would chide him with threats of hellfire or exhort him with visions of celestial reward, it had little impact, no more than the night-time monsters of a children's fairy tale would suffice to deter a criminal. And even when she warned him about becoming an 'infidel' and the terrible damnation that awaited such souls, she reiterated tenets mechanically, as if she were parroting someone else's dogma, catechizing him as she herself had been coerced into belief.

What was worse, her religion never made her happy. But by the end of her life nothing did, and she watched over Hasan as if from a sense of duty, not because it gave her any real joy to do so. Though if the truth were known, she had loved him dearly but with a heart too seared with pain to love him wisely.

Living with such a person day in and day out had exacted a heavy toll on Hasan. His feelings, his personal thoughts, his fears and longings, all were secreted deep within. He wanted to believe in something more, something encompassing, something that could explain injustice and the cruelty of people toward one another. But even in his short life he had come to distrust religion and the fanaticism it could bring, evil done in the name of God. It hardly enticed him to believe in a loving God, if God could indulge in such mischief.

He had never discussed these thoughts — he didn't dare. He stayed to himself, a frail spirit in an even frailer body, like the fruit of a malnourished tree. The tender acceptance of his Aunt Nahid and Uncle Husayn had awakened something else within him, a thought that perhaps his own parents had been like them, full of joy and laughter, strong and positive. And as the wagon jostled along the lake road, he wondered whether, if his parents had lived, he might have been strong, happy and bright like his cousin Ali.

The three talked little as the wagon made its way from Tiberias toward the Yarmuk River valley where the village of 'Adasíyyih flourished with its magnificent climate and fertile soil. It was still quite early, the sun just beginning to rise above the Golan. The sound of the wagon wheels crunching stones and the gentle rhythm of water lapping the shore mingled with the shrill cry of gulls dancing in the wind, swooping down to fetch minnows which swam innocently beneath the tranquil surfaces of this ancient lake.

Wedged between Moayyed on his right and Ali, who now held the reins, Hasan studied his cousin's face. He wanted to be like him. He was not jealous of Ali's physical appearance exactly, not the strong dark face, tanned from hours out in the small dinghy, a young man on the verge of adulthood, his face already showing traces of a beard. No, it was something inside, a conviction, a spirit, a happiness — that was what he envied.

This morning the mid-winter breeze of the lake was quite chilly, but the sun, low as it was in the southern sky, felt warm on Hasan's face. He pondered the analogy Moayyed had used the night before, about how the moon was but the means by which the sun conveyed its qualities to the earth. He tried for an instant to look directly at the sun, but could not. He wondered about the sun. What was it, after all, this source of all light and life, of warmth and nourishment?

By lunchtime they had travelled the ten or twelve kilometres from Tiberias to the bridge crossing over the river. To their right were rich fields and farmland, watered by the Jordan River, the Yawneel River and the Yarmuk. Ahead of them the road rose upward into a gorge that split the hills, dividing the Golan on the left from the mountains of Gilead.

'Tonight we will stay at the home of a family that lives near the hot mineral springs,' said Moayyed. He proceeded to describe to them his lifelong friendship with Hormoz, an old man like himself who lived alone in a simple cottage. Most of his own family were dead — the rest were scattered — so he helped young Persian immigrants by having them live with him until they had the means to build a place of their own.

Early in the afternoon they arrived at the Hammat Gader, the hot springs which for centuries the ailing had visited, believing in the healing properties of these mineral-rich waters. The settlement consisted of a few small farmhouses near the springs themselves. On either side the hills rose up from the deep gorge that the river had cut through the rock. As the river rose up to the springs and beyond, it twisted and turned, forming many waterfalls and hanging gardens, a spectacular sight for Ali and Hasan, who immediately began to speak of exploring these beautiful sites.

'I didn't bring you here for a holiday,' Moayyed cautioned them, but the tone of his voice let them know that, in fact, this was exactly why he had let them come along.

Soon they reached the small house where lived Moayyed's old and trusted friend, Hormoz Jalali. He was not as old as Moayyed and had no beard. In his small two-room cottage lived a Parsee Bahá'í couple, who had journeyed from Persia to be near 'Abdu'l-Bahá and to help with the growing of crops in 'Adasíyyih.

The couple were in their twenties and said little. The young man, Habib, had just come in from working in the fields all day, for even though it was winter, there was much to be done. Ferodeh, the young wife, had already prepared a most elaborate array of vegetables and lentils with a spicy sauce.

After brief greetings and introductions, the two young cousins eagerly sat down to eat and hardly looked up from their food. There was little conversation that evening. Everyone was exhausted. Hasan and Ali slept on thin pallets on a stone floor, but the constant sound of water coursing down the river toward the Jordan valley below made such a hypnotic sound that sleep came quickly.

The next morning Moayyed had work to do, he said, and the boys would have to take care of themselves, which they knew was his way of saying they could explore the waterfall and climb around on some of the less treacherous rock formations. They wandered along the twisting pathways until they discovered a place like nothing either of them had seen before. They climbed down a narrow trail that wound among scrub bushes and small trees towards the Yarmuk River itself. And the closer they got to the river, the larger were the trees and the louder the water.

The last hundred metres the trail was completely covered over by several large sycamore trees, relics of a past age before men had stripped the land of this precious commodity. The force of the water pouring over a precipice and pounding into the deep pool below it made such thunder that the boys could feel the vibrations of the noise through their feet. Hasan, who was not really used to the out-of-doors and certainly had never walked in terrain like this, felt nervous but excited by the venture. Ali liked nothing better than exploring the wild — to him this was paradise on earth.

Soon they had made their way down to the lower pool where there were several large rocks to sit on. The morning sun shone from above the waterfall down through the trees. The churning water was foamy and white, but the water around the edges of the pool was crystal clear and they could see an occasional fish darting near where they sat.

'Bahá'u'lláh loved to walk in the countryside,' said Ali. 'He spent almost two years in the mountains of Sulaymáníyyih.'

Hasan said nothing. He was watching the water tumble from the top of the waterfall, which was at least fifteen or twenty metres high. He tried to single out one drop and follow it from the summit to the pool below, but it always got lost in the foam.

The boys sat and watched for almost an hour, occasionally skipping a small flat river rock across the surface of the pool. Then Hasan unexpectedly said to Ali, 'You are very lucky, you know.'

'Lucky? In what way?'

'You have such confidence about what you think. I guess it's the way you were brought up.' He meant it as a compliment, but it sounded as if Hasan thought Ali had not really considered his own beliefs, that he had merely inherited the beliefs of his parents.

'I was not always so confident,' said Ali, thinking about the years before when he had spent most of a spring and summer trying to discover exactly what it meant to call himself a Bahá'í. 'It's easy to have a name, to call yourself a Bahá'í or anything else,' said Ali. 'But even if you are brought up to believe something, eventually you have to make it your own.'

'You sound like you have thought about it very carefully.'

'I have,' said Ali quickly, 'I have.'

There was silence for a while, then Hasan said what had been on his mind in the first place.

'I sometimes wonder if God really exists,' he said, looking at the waterfall. It was not an easy thing to admit, and it was only his regard for his slightly older cousin that gave him the courage to admit his doubt.

Ali was taken aback. He had grown up aware on some level that his own beliefs were different from those of the majority of people in 'Akká, but even they professed belief in God. And even when he had doubted his own beliefs as a Bahá'í, he had always communicated with God in prayer, had always felt as sure of the reality of God as anything else he knew or understood.

'When I see beautiful places like this, or when I see the stars in the night sky, I feel that there must be something, something that under-stands what is happening,' said Hasan, 'but . . . but I can't really say I know what that force is like.'

He paused, trying to think of the words which would say what he really meant. 'For one thing, if God is so powerful and good, the way my grandmother used to describe Him, then why can't we see Him or hear Him? Why must it be so hard to believe in Him? Why are you so sure there is a God?'

Because he had always accepted the existence of God as a funda-mental truth, Ali had never considered the question before and it caused him to think very hard, to be objective about something which was simply part of what he had always believed.

'I suppose I know there is a God the same way I know anything else,' he said at last.

'But you know about other things because you see them or touch them or hear them. Do you believe in God simply because you are told it is true?'

Ali was silent for what seemed like a very long time, then he looked at the endless flow of water pounding down the rock face. 'Do you think that water will ever stop?' he asked Hasan.

'What?' asked his confused cousin.

'The water rushes down into the pool hour after hour, day after day. Why doesn't it run dry?'

'Because the water flows from the mountains and hills. It begins with rain or springs, then collects in small tributaries. These gather into streams that form the river.'

'But the Yarmuk is a short river, only a few kilometres long. Where does all this take place?'

'Above us,' said Hasan, 'in the hills of Gilead to the right and the Golan to the left.'

'Have you ever seen these places?' asked Ali.

'No,' said Hasan.

'Have you even seen pictures of them?'

'No.'

'Yet you believe in them.'

'I know I could see them if I wanted to.'

'Do you think you will ever climb that mountain to see if you are correct?'

'No,' said Hasan smiling, 'I can promise you that.'

'Yet you have faith that you are correct.'

'Well, you may call it faith if you wish, but I am very certain of it.'

'It is not a *blind* faith, you mean.'

'No. I have studied science enough to know that water doesn't come from nothing; it comes from the earth or from clouds, and collects and flows according to the law of gravity.'

'There you go — that's the point. That's how I feel about believing in God. I feel no more need to see or touch God than you do to visit the springs of the Yarmuk. It is true that my parents taught me about God as I was growing up, just as they taught me about rivers and streams and other facts of this life. But just as you have had experiences that convince you there really is a law of gravity, I have experiences that convince me that what they taught me about God is completely true.'

'What sorts of experiences?' asked Hasan.

'Prayer, for one thing. Whenever I pray about something, I become aware of the results of my prayer.'

'Perhaps the results would have happened anyway.'

'No. No, it's not just something that happens once in awhile. It happens consistently in ways that I know are related to the prayer.'

'Can you prove that?'

'You mean in the same way that you prove something in science or maths?'

'Yes.'

'It doesn't work that way. Look, if I could take out a sheet of paper and prove to you that there is a God, what would that mean to you?'

'What do you mean?'

'Would you feel better or happier? Would you have faith in God?'

'Perhaps.'

'But it wouldn't answer your question, would it? You still wouldn't know why God is concealed from us in this life. You still wouldn't know what God is like, would you?'

'No,' said Hasan with a smile, recognizing that Ali was correct, that Ali had understood the heart of what was bothering him. 'No, you're right.'

'It is possible to prove that God exists — at least, I've heard Grandfather discuss it, but that's not what I mean about proof. I didn't decide to believe in God because it seemed like a good thing to do or because someone proved to me on a piece of paper that God exists. Knowing that there is a God has been as much a part of my life as everything else I know, and like everything else I know, it depends on many kinds of evidence.'

He considered what might explain what he meant. 'When I study history,' he said finally, 'I see how the advent of the Manifestations has shaped the course of history. When I see the strength of the Bahá'ís who have faced death, people like your own parents, I know that there had to be a source of assistance outside themselves. Or when I study the teachings of the Prophets, I can see that even though they lived thousands of years apart, they are united in everything they say – that similarity can't be simply a coincidence.'

Ali stopped. 'I'm talking too much,' he said with a smile.

'I don't mind,' said Hasan. 'I want to know what you think.'

The statement embarrassed Ali because it clearly revealed his cousin's respect for him. Yet there was no hint of jealousy or disdain in Hasan's voice because there was none in his heart.

Suddenly a large bird came wheeling out of the sky, folded its wings and plummeted to a limb of a tree beside the waterfall. Intent on watching the fish that swam in the pool at the bottom of the falls, the bird was oblivious to the two boys. The limb at first bobbed up and down with the sheer weight of the bird.

'Look!' whispered Hasan as he tugged at Ali's sleeve. The two did not move, but watched the hunter measure its prey. The eyes blinked, then with one swift gesture it left its perch and hurled its body like a javelin at the water, then swooped up from the surface with a wriggling silver fish in its deft talons.

For several minutes the boys could talk of nothing else as they rehearsed each movement of what they had witnessed.

'Who could have believed it?' asked Hasan.

'That was the point I was trying to make,' said Ali. 'You could describe such a thing in great detail to someone who had never seen it, but unless he has seen the power and beauty of such a bird, he might have trouble believing that such a large creature could fly, much less perform such aerial acrobatics, even if you could show him scientifically how it could happen.'

'Then belief in God is something you simply have to accept?'

'No, no. That's not what I mean. It is not a matter of just deciding you will do it or experience it, and it is not an accident, something you catch, like a bad cold, nor is it something you inherit, like an heirloom, or something you can be commanded to do.'

'Then how does it happen?' asked Hasan.

As Ali was struggling for an answer, a sudden breeze rushed over-head, bending the tops of the sycamore, yet because the boys were down in the gorge, they could not feel any wind at all. Hasan re-marked how strange it was to hear the wind and see it and not feel it.

'You need to feel the wind to understand truly what it is,' said Ali. 'That's what I mean, I guess, that it is not enough to observe its ef-fects or prove what it can do. Mr Bushrú'í said once that the essence of conviction is independent investigation of truth, and 'Abdu'l-Bahá said that if belief is contrary to the standards of science, it is mere superstition and will fail. But my mother explained the whole thing to me once in a simple way I've never forgotten.'

'What was that?'

'She asked me to imagine that there was a girl in Tasmania who was deeply in love with me.' Hasan listened eagerly with a grin. 'She said, "Ali, this girl would die for you, would give you everything she owns." Then she stopped and said, "Now, how does that make you feel?"'

'Well, I had to admit that I was a little flattered, but the more I thought about it, the more I had to confess it did not mean a great deal since I had never met the girl or received her gifts. Mother went on to explain to me that belief in God is much the same. It is not enough that we be told that God exists or that God loves us. We must search for that love, discover it acting in our lives, and nurture it.

'It was shortly afterwards that I had the marvellous dream I told you about.'

'The one about the horse and flying over 'Akká?'

'Exactly. That's when I began to study, really study, about being a Bahá'í.'

'But weren't you raised as a Bahá'í?'

'Yes, but I wanted my beliefs to be mine, not simply something I did or thought because I should. I saw what joy was in the hearts of those who had discovered the Faith of Bahá'u'lláh on their own, and I envied them that excitement. I wanted to know that same feeling.

Do you understand what I mean? Naturally it was assumed that because my parents are Bahá'ís, I would be a Bahá'í as well, but I knew that if I assumed the same thing, if I allowed myself to be called a Bahá'í simply because my parents are Bahá'ís, my beliefs would mean little to me or to anyone else.

'After all,' Ali continued, 'some of the closest members of the family of Bahá'u'lláh and 'Abdu'l-Bahá became the most inveterate enemies of the Faith, the chief Covenant-breakers. If belief could be inherited, then what happened to them? That frightened me when I first thought about it. I knew then the only way to protect myself against such mischief would be to find out for myself exactly what it means to be a Bahá'í.'

'Weren't you a little young to be worried about things like that?' asked Hasan.

'Tell me, Hasan, how long have you been thinking about God and why people do the things they do in the name of religion?'

'As long as I can remember,' Hasan confessed, 'though I couldn't put it into words.'

'Now you can,' said Ali. 'And because you can put the questions into words, you can discover the answers.'

'Perhaps so,' said Hasan. 'Perhaps I can after all.'

They talked awhile longer, but not so much about belief or God. Instead they waited to see if the bird would return or if they could spy any other creatures whose secret ways they might observe. Toward late afternoon, they became fascinated by the large fish feeding in the deep mountain pool. As they were leaving, Hasan jokingly turned to the pool, tossed a pebble into the deep green water and said, 'So long, fish!' Before the words were out of his mouth, a large sleek trout breached the slick surface, turned a flip as if to bid adieu, then splashed back into the pond.

4

An Island in Space

THAT evening a cold wind swept through the valley, and the
crowded stucco cottage felt draughty indeed. But inside, the
boys gathered with the two older men and the young couple
around a small but brightly-kindled hearth.

Neither the husband nor the wife spoke much, and Moayyed and
his host talked mostly about the prospects for a good crop and getting
the food to Haifa and 'Akká where it would be in increasingly short
supply if the war dragged on. Ali and Hasan were joking about the
fish who had bid them farewell at the pool when Moayyed turned to
them and said, 'So that's where you were all morning when everyone
else was hard at work?'

'It's a holiday,' said Ali.

'Don't think because you are away from home you are on a holiday
— tomorrow you go to school.'

'Where?' asked Hasan.

'At Maryam's,' said Hormoz with a grin.

'But she teaches little children,' said Ali, remembering vividly years
before when he had been one of Maryam's 'victims', as he jokingly
said to his parents. As was the custom, in the classes for older children,
the boys were separated from the girls, though even the older children
were taught by Bahá'ís in the village since there was no other school.

Many of the children of villagers who were not Bahá'ís also gratefully attended the classes. But Maryam taught young children – between seven and nine – both boys and girls, and over the years she had acquired quite a reputation for her sometimes unorthodox methods of instruction.

'And what's wrong with teaching children?' asked Moayyed.

'I'm no longer a child, Grandfather,' said Ali in disbelief.

'Who said anything about your being a student?' Moayyed turned away to sip his tea. 'You and Hasan are going to help her teach!'

'Oh, no!' said Ali. 'It was hard enough being her student; now I have to work for her?'

'Please, sir,' said Hasan, a little unnerved by the suggestion, 'I'm not qualified to teach children about the Bahá'í Faith; I understand only a little about it myself.'

'You'll do fine,' Hormoz reassured Hasan. 'Just do what she says and you'll be fine.'

'Do what she says or else!' said Ali.

'True, quite true,' said Moayyed, still nonchalant about the whole thing. 'Well, since you didn't work today, what did you do? We did not have fish for dinner, so I assume you did not go fishing.'

'We talked,' said Hasan.

'I see,' said Moayyed.

'About God,' the boy continued.

'And what did you conclude?' asked Ferodeh. Hasan looked at her kind face and dark eyes. She was not extraordinarily beautiful, but there was something exceptional in her gracious manner, a quality of kindness and inner strength.

'We decided that knowing God is a very personal thing,' said Ali, 'not something you can really prove.'

'Oh?' said Ferodeh. 'How very wise of you. But how did you decide that?'

Hasan related the essence of their discussion, and when he had finished, the adults commended Ali on his response to Hasan's questions. Then to the surprise of Hormoz, Ferodeh, who rarely joined in on their conversations, said, 'It is true that proof means little to a closed heart, but the proofs are there. Eventually scientists will discover God in spite of themselves, just as people of religion will replace superstition with the standards of science.'

Hormoz was shocked. The young couple had lived with him for three months, and though they had been most pleasant and gracious guests, he had never heard either of them say much about their beliefs.

'She's absolutely correct,' said Moayyed. 'I have heard the Master say that "religion must be in conformity with science and reason, so that it may influence the hearts of men. The foundation must be solid and must not consist of imitations."'

'Yes,' Ferodeh agreed, 'He has even gone so far as to say, "If a question be found contrary to reason, faith and belief in it are impossible and there is no outcome but wavering and vacillation."'

Again Hormoz was startled by the young woman's knowledge, but her husband Habib smiled at the expression he saw on his friend's face. 'Simple farmers can read too, eh?' he said, and sipped his tea.

For the briefest moment there was silence, then a snicker from Ali, then laughter from everyone. 'Indeed, indeed,' said Hormoz.

'If you wish,' said Ferodeh, 'there is a sort of game an uncle of mine played with me once – we could all do it. It requires a great deal of imagination, but it once helped me understand one sort of proof of the existence of God.'

'A proof of God?' asked Hasan with interest.

'Somewhat,' said Ferodeh, 'but more, really – an analogy that has always helped me understand how God assists us. And isolated as we are here with the winter wind whistling through the door, it would not require a great deal of imagination after all.'

'Let's do it!' said Ali.

'I'm game,' said Hormoz.

'As long as I don't have to dance or sing,' said Moayyed.

'Dance only if you want to,' said Ferodeh with a laugh.

'He doesn't,' said Ali quickly. 'Believe me, he doesn't!'

'Very well,' said Ferodeh. 'First you must all gather your chairs close together in a circle.'

All obliged and slid the chairs tightly together in the flickering light. Someone looking in the small windows might have assumed this to be some clandestine meeting instead of a game.

'We are on an island,' Ferodeh began in an animated voice, 'an island far out in the very middle of the ocean.'

'What ocean?' asked Ali.

'We don't know its name', said Ferodeh, 'because we have never seen any other land, nor do we know how we got here.'

'We must have sailed here,' said Hasan.

'We don't know how to sail, nor do we know how to build boats,' said Ferodeh.

'I do!' said Ali.

'Not on our island you don't,' said Ferodeh.

'Does the island have a name?' asked Hasan.

'Would you like it to have a name?' asked Ferodeh.

'Of course,' said Hasan, his interest growing the more his imagination began to build this island in his mind. 'Let's call it Hasanland.'

'Good name,' said Moayyed.

'A nice sound to it,' Hormoz agreed.

'Very well, then, Hasanland it is,' said Ferodeh. 'Now, we have several problems in Hasanland, very important problems at that.'

'Like what?' asked Hasan.

'For one thing, the island is very small, barely large enough for all of us.'

'So is this house,' said Hormoz, 'but we seem to do all right.'

'Now, now,' said Ferodeh. 'You must forget about this house. You must forget everything you know and enter Hasanland with your whole heart.'

'What other problems do we have?' asked Hasan.

'We have no language or skills to speak of because, one and all, we have no recollection of our past.'

'Then how shall we survive?' asked Ali. 'What shall we eat and how shall we live?'

'That is the problem,' said Ferodeh. 'Here we are with all this potential and we must somehow find a way to get by.'

'Ali and I could gather the food,' said Hasan.

'How will you know what is edible, what is nourishing or what is poisonous?' asked Habib. 'Not only that, but since you cannot talk, how will you agree to do anything?'

'We can make clothes from straw,' said Ali. 'I have seen pictures of tribes that wear such things.'

'But what about Hormoz and me?' said Moayyed. 'We are so old that I fear we would be of no help whatsoever in Hasanland.'

'Don't be silly, sir,' said Hasan. 'You know so much — you could be our teacher. You could tell us how to get along.'

'Not in Hasanland,' said Moayyed. 'I am afraid we are without assistance.'

'But how can we build a shelter? What will we do if it gets cold or if it rains?'

'We can learn these things,' said Hormoz. 'The people on this earth did not know everything in the beginning. They learned, little by little, even though it took aeons for mankind to ascend from darkness and ignorance.'

'There's a problem with that,' said Habib again. 'We don't have aeons — if we don't survive, no one will remain to learn.'

'There's an even more significant problem, I fear,' said Moayyed, becoming more and more caught up in the spirit of this exercise.

'What's that, Grandfather?' asked Ali.

'Now I think I understand the true nature of our dilemma.'

'What?' asked Hasan.

'I can't tell you because we don't have speech.'

'Let him speak, Ferodeh,' said Ali.

'I permit it,' said Ferodeh with a laugh.

'Very well,' said Moayyed. 'Useless though I be in this crude land.'

'Please,' said Hasan in mock seriousness, 'you're talking about my namesake.'

'Pardon me,' said Moayyed, 'but you'll have to admit it does not seem to be a very propitious place to live right now, especially now that I see the heart of the dilemma Ferodeh has created for us. You see, scientists are now formulating what are called the laws of thermodynamics, laws which state that in a closed system, which our island is, energy, even spiritual and intellectual energy, cannot come from nothing. Or to put it another way, we can hope to become no brighter, to ascend no higher than the best of us on the island, and unfortunately, none of us has any knowledge of anything better than what we already are . . .'

'Which is miserable,' said Ali.

'Exactly,' said Moayyed.

'But people are creative,' said Hasan. 'People have new ideas all the time. What about inventors and writers? Why can't we simply use our imaginations and invent whatever we need?'

'Because', Hormoz offered, 'even the imagination must be primed.' He pointed to the hand pump which pulled up water from the well for cooking and drinking. 'That pump is a most useful device. Without it we would not have any water. But until we prime the pump, until we put water down it and then crank the handle, it is simply an awkwardly-shaped hunk of metal.'

'Or take a flower,' said Ferodeh. 'A flower gives us beautiful blossoms, but not until energy and nourishment are poured into the flower — the sunlight, the water, the minerals in the soil.'

'But people are not like flowers,' said Hasan. 'People don't depend on what is given to them — they can go out and find what they need. People have brains.'

'That's true,' said Ali. 'But even people need to be taught to use their brains, to set them in motion.'

'And so far', said Moayyed, 'no one on our island has the slightest idea how to begin.'

'We'll pray about it,' Hasan suggested.

'We don't know how to pray,' said Ferodeh. 'We don't know speech or words, nor do we know about God.' All were silent as they examined their baffling situation. Hasan squirmed in his chair, then looked at the ceiling.

'Unless we have some outside assistance, we're doomed,' said Ali, shaking his head.

'Very well, then,' said Ferodeh. 'We shall have a helper, a visitor from another land. He arrives in his small boat. He knows a great deal.'

'Then he can teach us,' said Hasan.

'Except we won't be able to understand him,' Ali reminded them.

'He will be kind and understanding,' said Habib. 'He will appreciate our pitiful condition and will gradually teach us to speak and perhaps how to feed and clothe ourselves.'

'The problem is,' said Ferodeh, 'will we recognize him as a teacher, as a superior person? He may seem strange to us. He may dress differently, and because he can talk, we may think he is possessed. We may be afraid of him instead of welcoming him as our teacher.'

'Then he will have to be a most understanding and astute teacher,' said Hormoz.

'But it will take so long,' said Hasan. 'It has taken me thirteen years to learn what I know . . .'

'What you used to know,' Ferodeh reminded him.

'Yes, yes, I forgot — what I used to know. But how can we learn everything we need? Think how long it took before mankind learned how to make a printing press, or a car — that's a recent invention. How are we going to learn everything?'

'It would take time,' said Ferodeh. 'It may be that it would take generations to be taught everything.'

'In which case we would have to have more than one teacher,' said Ali.

'I think we would,' said Ferodeh.

'But why is that?' asked Hasan.

'Because', said Ferodeh, 'we can learn only so much at one time, and there is no end to how much we need to learn.'

'Perhaps an example would make it clearer,' said Habib. 'I am a farmer. It has taken me twenty years to learn what I know now about farming, lessons learned from the time I was a boy at my father's side. And yet there is always more to learn, new techniques, new tools being developed. If I came to you tomorrow and said, "Hasan, I am going to teach you about farming today," how would you feel?'

'Excited,' said Hasan.

'But what if I insisted that I would teach you everything I knew in one day.'

'That would be impossible,' said Hasan. 'If it took you twenty years, I couldn't possibly do it.'

'No matter how much you desired to learn or how hard I tried to teach you?'

'No,' Hasan admitted.

'Perhaps I could skip over the less important things and concern myself only with teaching you advanced techniques in producing high yields of wheat.'

'I still couldn't do it. I don't know the first thing about planting or ploughing a field. I would have no idea where to begin!'

'Well, I am a very busy farmer – perhaps I could simply teach you the first lesson and you could learn the rest on your own.'

'Nope,' Hasan said with a smile. 'I suppose in time I could figure some things out, but by that time I would have starved to death and ruined the fields.'

'Teaching is like that,' said Ferodeh. 'It's sometimes very frustrating. I used to teach young children in my village in Persia, and I remember how long it took me to learn patience at being satisfied with what they could learn for that one day. You see, I knew what capacity they had and I knew what I wanted them to learn, but if I pushed them too hard, even the little bit they might have learned that day was lost.'

'So we would need more than one teacher to come to our island,' said Hasan.

'Or else he would have to come more than one day,' said Ferodeh.

'When would he be able to stop coming?' asked Ali.

'What do you mean?' asked Ferodeh.

'When would we know enough so that we could do everything for ourselves – you know, make our clothes, build shelters, gather and raise food, all that?'

'Good question,' said Ferodeh. 'Let me answer it with a question for you. Take your life right now. When do you think you will have learned everything you need to know?'

'That's silly,' said Ali. 'I will never know *everything* I need to know.'

'Well, let me put it another way,' said Ferodeh. 'When do you think you will know enough not to need any more assistance in order to learn?'

'Assistance of what kind? You mean a teacher?'

'Any sort of help from outside yourself.'

'I think I will always need that in some way or another,' said Ali.

'Then perhaps that's our answer for the island as well,' said Ferodeh. 'We will always need further instruction because we will never reach a point where we have reached the limit of our capacity to develop.'

'It's the same with my crops,' said Habib. 'No matter how well I have irrigated the fields and fertilized the plants and weeded and cared for the things I grow, they will still need more nurturing tomorrow – more water, more sun.'

'Then it is established,' said Moayyed. 'In Hasanland, we will need some assistance from elsewhere or we shall be doomed to starve, freeze and live in general misery. And perhaps when he comes, this teacher can provide some useful tasks for old men,' he said, winking at Hormoz.

'But what about our imaginations?' said Hasan, still not convinced that they could not manage on their own, or at least with fewer teachers. 'Could we not take what the teacher says and improvise? Would he have to be constantly there to tell us what to do?'

'He might leave a book of instructions for us to follow – how to build a hut, how to weave cloth – after he has taught us to read, of course. Is that what you mean?'

'More than that, really. After all, people invent things – why couldn't we help ourselves through some of this.'

'You mean you would find it more satisfying to figure out some of the answers to our situation without simply following instructions?'

'Yes,' said Hasan.

'Me too,' said Ali.

'Very well,' said Ferodeh. 'We will have to be sure that our teacher is not too oppressive, that he gives us a choice. Perhaps instead of telling us *exactly* what to do, the teacher could give us clues, hints, suggestions, and then we would have to figure out the rest for ourselves.'

'I like that,' said Hasan.

'I am glad these young people like the challenge,' said Moayyed. 'Perhaps they can do all the hard work and let us old people lie in our hammocks and eat dates and pomegranates.'

'No such luck,' said Ferodeh. 'As time passes on our island, the old will be the historians, the repositories of wisdom. From them we will learn whether our new ideas have any merit because they will have seen ideas come and go.'

'Good, good,' said Hormoz. 'I like to feel useful, even in Hasanland.'

'Do we have it then?' asked Ferodeh. 'Do we have what we need to survive in Hasanland?'

'Not just survive,' said Hasan. 'We will prosper and advance.'

'And do you, Hasan, understand what this island represents?'

'The earth,' he said.

'That's right − the earth is an island in space.'

'And the teachers,' said Hasan, 'they are the Manifestations, the Prophets?'

'True,' said Ferodeh. 'You see, 'Abdu'l-Bahá says that without the Manifestations there would be no progress on earth.'

'I remember once 'Abdu'l-Bahá compared the advent of the Prophets to the coming of spring,' said Habib. 'He said that after the winter when plants wither, the herbs fade, the garden becomes a dust-heap, the spring comes with warm sun, showers, and the renewal of life. It is the same when the Prophets appear.'

'You mean that without the Manifestations, humankind would not learn anything?' asked Hasan.

'How could we?' said Ferodeh. 'The human family is no different from our island family. A child needs a fair upbringing and tender nurturing in order to survive, let alone prosper. A child left to its own devices will surely perish. A child whose physical needs are met but who is deprived of education will be little better than a beast of the field. And those who have been well fostered in all aspects, who are set in motion toward human perfection, even they must receive physical, mental and spiritual sustenance daily.'

'Remember my plants?' said Habib to Hasan. 'People are the same. No matter how well you ate two or three days ago, you must have nourishment again. It is the same with spiritual nourishment. No matter how fervently you prayed yesterday or how nobly you acted, you need more spiritual sustenance today in order to meet the new challenges confronting you and produce yet more noble deeds.'

'But how does the game of the island prove there is a God?' asked Hasan.

'It is very simple,' said Ferodeh. 'If you admit that people left without education or assistance would remain ignorant, surviving only as the animals of the wilderness survive, only not as well, per-haps − then the very fact that we are here now talking about the complex affairs of civilization means that humanity long ago emerged from that condition. Something must have occurred, correct? Therefore, humankind must have received assistance to come as far as it has.'

Hasan smiled at the logical end of what had been both a game and a proof, and he felt a profound sense of communion among his fellow inhabitants of the fictive island. The others felt the same sort of satis-faction and, as if on cue, everyone became silent, contented with Ferodeh's adventure and beginning to feel how really tired they were from their day's labour.

Hasan looked at the fire, its flames now nearly gone. A piece of a log, seemingly bleak and cold fell through the grate and broke open on the hearth into bright embers of red and orange. Yellow and blue sparks shot from it as resins crackled in the heat. Soon the fire would need more wood, another thick log to warm the cold night in Hasanland.

The orphaned boy looked at the other faces, tired from the day's labour, but peaceful, contented. Like him, they watched the fire, and the dying flame reflected in their eyes. Perhaps this was his family now, these cohabitants of Hasanland, these simple souls unknown to the world at large, huddled together in a stone hut in Galilee. They were so distant from the flashing cannon that struck like thunder over the battlefields of Europe, ploughing its earth with the tools of war, nurturing the sod with the blood of misguided humanity.

So remote they were, yet one on this small island in space — the victors and the victims, the farmers of Galilee and the soldiers conscripted from their own small villages, then sent by kings and emperors who had too little wisdom to heed the advice of their latest teacher come to guide them through guideless times.

But the emperor's day would soon be done. The glare of battlefields, like the fire's embers, would soon dim and be gone. The kings would vanish and their gaudy houses of crystal and gold become museums, totems of archaic notions of how the world should be served. Meanwhile, the island, like a bud packed tight in early spring, was about to burst forth in bloom, and some of its inhabitants, like Ferodeh and Habib, sensed the imminence of that change.

5

Maryam and the Junkroom Game

MARYAM was a sturdy woman in her forties. She had been quite attractive in her youth, but in the storm of persecution that swept through the Bahá'í community in Persia she had put aside concerns for her appearance and family matters. The family that had once been hers was painfully gone — now her sole concern was educating the children of the families in 'Adasíyyih. This was her life's work.

It would not be wrong to say that the children of 'Adasíyyih were in awe of Maryam — they never knew what sort of unusual activity she would have them doing in her classes. And because they never knew what to expect, they were always alert, always slightly nervous, at least until the class got started and they became thoroughly engrossed in the method of her madness.

She lived by herself in a small and simple cottage that had built onto it a large makeshift room where the classes were held, and though she kept to herself and was not what one would call a very social sort of person, she was greatly loved and admired by everyone, especially by the parents of small children.

Ali and Hasan arrived early the next morning, about an hour before the children arrived, thinking they might have to sweep the room or help in some other way. Hasan was understandably apprehensive as Ali drove the carriage to the top of a small knoll where the house was perched like a beacon of hope.

Ali expected her to be up and about, out in the yard feeding her goats, or cleaning — she was always cleaning. But she was nowhere to be seen. The two tied the team beneath a large tree in front of the house. They walked up to the door of the classroom, knocked, but there was no answer and the unlocked door swung open. They walked inside, but she was not there, and the chairs Ali expected to be neatly in a circle were chaotically scattered as if the room had been devastated by a storm or marauding thieves.

The boys looked at each other with concern. Ali had told Hasan stories about how the Arab tribes used to raid the village. What if Maryam had been hurt? What if the raiders were still there waiting to attack them as well?

They walked softly to the back of the room, each contemplating how he might respond to a sudden onslaught or the sight of Maryam's maimed body.

Suddenly they heard a moan, a soft, repeated sound like the call of a morning dove, only irregular and broken. It was coming from inside the doorway at the back left of the room which led into Maryam's kitchen. They stepped quietly, peered around the door frame and saw the long dress of Maryam's kneeling body, in pain? In agony?

'Haji, Haji, Haji,' she cooed, her back to the boys, her right arm moving in a strange stroking pattern.

'Khanum?' said Ali in an uncertain tone.

'Oh!' exclaimed the startled woman, spinning around so fast she dropped the saucer of goat's milk which she was feeding to her cat Haji. The grey, long-haired cat hissed as it jumped from the floor to the top of a cupboard in one leap.

'My goodness,' she said, pulling herself up with the help of Hasan's extended hand, 'you startled me so; I did not hear you come in.'

'When we saw the chairs and everything scattered around the classroom, we were afraid something had happened,' said Ali.

'Arab raiders!' said Hasan.

'I see, I see,' she said, straightening her dress and going into the classroom. 'So you came to save me, did you?' Ali blushed. 'And what would you have done, said "Boo!" to them?'

The boys laughed and Ali introduced himself and his cousin Hasan to Maryam, explaining that they had come to help her. She welcomed them both, said she remembered Ali from his first visit, and went on to explain why the room was in such disarray. 'We're going to play the junkroom game,' she said.

'I don't think I remember that one,' said Ali.

'I've never heard of a game like that,' said Hasan.

'Well, I'm not surprised,' said Maryam, stroking the cat which, having become assured that all was well, had wandered into the room to be with Maryam. 'I invented it a year ago, so I doubt that the rest of the world is familiar with it yet.'

'Do you want us to straighten up the room?' asked Hasan.

'No, no,' she said a little impatiently. 'This is to be the junkroom, understand? Did you really think I was such a horrible housekeeper as this?'

'Well, I . . .'

'Come, come,' she said, whisking up the cat into her arms, 'let me feed Haji and you two can have some tea. You will discover how the game is played soon enough.'

As the three sat at Maryam's table, she explained that she called the cat Haji because 'Abu'l-Qásim had found him at the Riḍván Garden. 'He was but a small kitten then, and 'Abu'l-Qásim had decided he was left behind by a family of cats on pilgrimage.'

The boys laughed at the story, and she continued talking about the village and the war and her young students. Hasan looked about the simple cottage at the abundance of pictures that covered the walls. Some were the faces of young children, others of young adults holding children of their own.

Maryam noticed Hasan's interest and explained that these were her most prized rewards for teaching. The young faces were former students and the photographs of the grown-ups beside them were the same students now grown. Most of the photographs were inscribed with heartfelt and touching sentiments: 'Thank you for helping me to discover myself', or, 'Thank you for making my beliefs come alive.' But what was clear in all of them was sincere gratitude, as if only now as adults, perhaps with children of their own, could they appreciate the extent of her influence on their development.

The pride Maryam felt in these trophies was evident in the care with which she arranged them on the wall and in the changed expression on her face when she spoke about them. Her usually brusque demeanour, so forbidding to her young charges, softened, and the tone of her voice revealed to Hasan the gentle and vulnerable soul behind the austere facade.

Maryam and the two boys talked a while longer. She asked Hasan about his trip from Persia, and she recalled Ali's previous visit to her classroom. She allowed Hasan to hold Haji – a prestigious honour indeed – then the young children began arriving from the village.

As a rule these youngsters were obedient, quiet, respectful, but when they saw the room in such disarray, they were shocked. Each had a special seat he or she usually occupied around the perimeter of a large circle, but the chairs were haphazardly arranged into a virtual maze and there was nothing for the students to do but stand and wait for Maryam's instruction.

Soon more than twenty students had arrived, and Maryam gathered them together near the doorway to the room where she had them sit on the floor. The children ranged in age from seven to ten – older village children attended other classes, or else worked in the fields with their parents.

'These are my assistants, Ali and Hasan,' said Maryam introducing the older boys to the children. She motioned for the two cousins to stand and be recognized. To their surprise, the class applauded politely. 'They will be helping us today on an adventure, a journey through the junkroom. But first, let us have our morning prayers.'

Without her saying another word, two students whose turn it was stood up in front of the others and proceeded to recite prayers and verses with remarkable clarity and inflection. When they were seated, Maryam explained the mystery of the room's confusion.

'Do you know what a junkroom is?' she began.

No one was quite sure.

'A junkroom is a place where we put all the things we don't use any more but are not yet ready to throw away. A junkroom may be a closet or an attic, a cellar, any place where such things might be stored.'

'But what kinds of things?' asked one child.

'A little of this and a little of that,' said Maryam.

'We keep all our old shoes in one box,' said a small girl.

'Old shoes make nice junk,' said Maryam.

'My father has many old shirts,' said a young boy.

'You see, junk can be all sorts of things, and after a few years the special place where we keep these things gets cluttered. And when we enter a junkroom and begin to sift through everything, we might discover some wonderful treasures.'

'I might find the doll I lost,' said one child.

'Perhaps so,' Maryam continued. 'But you may find bad surprises too − broken bottles or spiders.'

'Snakes!' Amin volunteered.

'Possibly. There might be snakes. In any case, today you will find out, because today this very room is a junkroom.'

'It is?' said Iraj.

'Most definitely.' She pointed to two chairs at the front of the room. 'There is the entrance and the two chairs at the back of the room are the exit.'

'But there's nothing in it!' said Shirin. 'Nothing except chairs.'

'Ah, but you see, those aren't ordinary chairs,' said Maryam, pointing to the chairs scattered throughout the room. 'These chairs are magic. Each chair can become whatever we desire in our special room − something wonderful like ... like ...', she scratched her head in mock serious meditation, waiting for some volunteer to complete the answer.

'Like a black Arabian stallion,' said Semira.

'Or a crystal palace,' said Ahmad.

'And yet there may be bad things too,' said Maryam, 'like ...'

'Like a hat full of bugs,' said Jamal.

'A pit of quicksand,' said Amin.

'But how do we know what the chair is?' asked Semira.

'On each chair there will be a piece of paper that will say exactly what the chair represents.'

'But I don't see any paper on them,' said Amin.

'True,' said Maryam, 'that will be your first part in this game.' She went on to explain that Ali would take one half of the group, Hasan the other, and each group would devise all sorts of intriguing items for the junkroom, some of them magnificent treasures, others useless or even dangerous.

Maryam made sure the maze of chairs was arranged just so while the two groups of children eagerly filled the room with imaginary surprises. There were huge boxes of sweetmeats, magic carpets, golden rings, palaces and sleek sailboats. But there were also boxes of broken glass, baskets of spiders, gardens of quicksand and poisonous blooms.

After a sizeable array of assorted ingredients had been collected by Hasan and Ali, Maryam took the two sets of papers, mixed them together thoroughly so that booty and traps were mingled randomly. Then she placed a single sheet on each of the chairs scattered throughout the room.

'Now', she said, her hands on her hips, 'I think we're quite ready to begin. Up here is the entrance,' she pointed to two chairs near the front of the room, 'and you leave through the two chairs at the other end. The idea of the junkroom game is simple enough – you try to leave with as many good things and as few bad things as you can. So we need a volunteer.' Several children immediately raised their hands. 'Not so fast,' she cautioned. 'First you need one important piece of equipment.' She pulled a bright red scarf from a pocket in her dress and held it up.

'What's that?' asked Amin, who had been the first to raise his hand.

'A blindfold,' said Maryam.

'Oooo,' said the children in a unanimous moan of disappointment.

'I'll volunteer,' said Amin, heedless of the handicap. 'My mother says I am blessed with good fortune.'

'Very well, my brave pilgrim,' said Maryam. She took Amin to the entrance and carefully blindfolded him. 'When you find a chair,' she instructed him, 'you must decide whether or not you wish to sit. If you choose to sit down, then the paper on that chair is yours. After you choose five chairs, you must exit, and we'll see what you gained on your journey through the junkroom.'

Whatever disappointment the children felt when they realized the treasures would not be so easily won was soon displaced by the thrill and mystery of chance. Would Amin get spiders or chocolates, an Arabian stallion or two rooms full of dishes to wash? At first the children were deathly quiet as they watched their compatriot awkwardly groping his way among the scattered chairs, choosing this one, forgoing that one, trying for all the world to appear as if he had some subtle instinct about which contained gold and which a pit of vipers.

But as he made his decisions, the group became more animated. They too began to feel that they knew what choices he should make, even though the writing on the papers was face down. Each decision evoked a blended assortment of cheers and groans so that by the end of his sojourn, the other students were as anxious as Amin to review the results of his choices.

When Amin exited, Ali helped remove the blindfold and Hasan collected the five sheets of paper.

'Now read them out,' said Maryam to Hasan.

'First, you have a castle on a mountain top,' said Hasan. Several 'ah's' followed. 'Next, the chocolates.' Even more 'ah's'. 'However, you have fallen into a tiger pit, have been stung by a nest of hornets, and have a dread disease which makes you allergic to candy.' A chorus of 'ugh's'.

Two more children ventured through the junkroom according to this same procedure, one doing exceptionally well — sitting on an anthill was his sole torture, while he garnered various sorts of fame and fortune for all his guessing. Then Maryam stopped the game and asked if they were pleased with how the game was proceeding.

Some were quite satisfied and wanted to continue, but one in particular, Semira, noted that there was, after all, not much skill required to sit in a chair, not much credit to be accrued for acquiring booty when all was left to chance.

'Quite so, quite so,' said Maryam, her finger to her lips, her eyes squinting as if in her puzzlement she was trying to devise a solution to the grievance. 'What if the wayfarer had some assistance,' she said. 'What if the wanderer had some information about the chair but still had to figure out if the information was correct?'

'Yes,' said Semira, 'that would be better.'

The others concurred, and so Maryam explained the revised rules. The student would still be blindfolded, but at each chair the pilgrim could hold up the paper for the others to see. They could not call out what it was, but they could indicate their opinion about the proper choice.

'Of course,' Maryam said with a sly look on her face and a wink, 'you cannot always trust these mischievous children, can you?' The other children took the hint, and after one of them had reached the second or third chair, the students were of no help whatever. The chorus of voices would be equally divided between those who would wholeheartedly endorse the choice, while an equally vociferous harangue issued dire warnings against it.

The end result was not much better than what the previous children had done. And after two more children tried these revised rules, they did even worse.

'My goodness,' said Maryam once more with her look of feigned bewilderment, 'this does not seem to help at all. If only these children were more reliable,' she said shaking her head.

'I have it,' she said, snapping her fingers. 'Come here, Hasan.' She pulled the boy to her, whispered something in his ear, then announced to the class, 'Hasan will be your guide. As you make your way through the junkroom, you may ask him whether the choice is good or bad.'

'He's going to trick us, you'll see,' said Amin.

'No, no,' said Semira, 'Maryam would not tell him to lie.'

'She told *us* to, didn't she?' said Amin.

'She did not!' Semira insisted indignantly. 'All of you simply decided it would be fun to do. That's how I ended up sitting on the anthill and falling in the tiger pit.'

The others laughed, but none was sure what Maryam had instructed Hasan. Was he to be trustworthy, devious, or capricious?

'I'll go first again,' said Amin, still the adventurous one, in spite of his initial failure.

'I'm afraid you get to go through the junkroom only once,' said Maryam.

'Ohhh,' said a disappointed boy.

'I'll go,' said Jamal, 'but can I ask him questions?'

'A few,' said Maryam.

So Jamal, less eagerly, put on the blindfold. He was led by Hasan to the starting place and quickly arrived at the first chair. He then handed the slip of paper to Hasan who, without revealing its contents to the children, said to Jamal, 'You should definitely take this one.' Jamal asked Hasan if he was certain. Hasan assured him it was a most wise decision, and there was not a hint of duplicity in his voice, no sign of dissimulation. Jamal plopped himself down in the chair.

And so it went with three of the other choices — Hasan would give his opinion and Jamal would follow it. But with the fifth chair, Jamal thought he heard one of the students snicker, and he wondered if perhaps they knew something he did not. He wondered if he had been utterly tricked, and his doubt swayed him. He promptly rejected Hasan's admonition not to sit, and with a vengeful smile sat down on top of a pillow full of poison needles.

When the accounting was made by Ali, the children were surprised to learn that except for the one unfortunate decision, Jamal fared the best of all. Quickly hands shot up with volunteers to go on the journey. Two more completed the trip, this time following Hasan's advice to the letter, and both had entirely successful ventures. Quickly those who had already gone longed to go once more.

Maryam smiled. 'No, no, what challenge is there now? You have all figured out that so long as you follow this trustworthy guide, this

guardian angel I have given you, you are perfectly secure and successful in your journey through the junkroom. You will reap all the
rewards and endure none of its pain.'

'Khanum,' said Semira, raising her hand.

'Yes, dear.'

'This isn't really a game about junkrooms, is it?'

'Whatever do you mean?' said Maryam, her heart swelling as she
watched her prize pupil solve yet another riddle that the subtle teacher
was forever devising to challenge her young students.

'The guide, Hasan, he represents the Manifestation, doesn't he?'

'Oh?' said Maryam. 'Why do you think so?'

The other children were suddenly looking again at the room.
Semira's suggestion got them thinking and suddenly several others
began to see in the simple game an analogy to life itself.

'Yes, yes,' said Amin. 'The entrance is birth and the exit is death.'

Others affirmed that the choices were the decisions one makes in life.
And so it went, the children not even waiting for Maryam to verify their
interpretation. They had been her students long enough to know that there
was ever a fine magic to her madness, a divine logic to her games.

When the suggestions ceased flowing and the major parts of the
analogy were resolved, Maryam smiled broadly. 'You are all too
bright for me,' she said. 'It is time for you to teach me.'

The students laughed, while Ali and Hasan watched in awe the
gems of wit and wisdom that Maryam had discovered in these precious mines.

'How could we teach *you* anything?' asked Amin.

'Well,' said Maryam, 'one thing puzzles me still. At the end of the
journey your papers were gathered and the success of the journey was
determined. What do you think that represents?'

Again Semira's hand shot up.

'Yes, Semira?'

'Does it have anything to do with the Hidden Word we learned last
week, the one which says, "Bring thyself to account each day ere thou
art summoned to a reckoning; for death, unheralded, shall come
upon thee and thou shalt be called to give account for thy deeds."'

'Ah, so the collection and reading of the papers is the accounting!' said Maryam. 'Thank you, Semira. But there's one more thing that I don't understand. This is actually a classroom, not a junkroom, correct?'

The students agreed in unison. 'Yes, Khanum.'

'And yet in a classroom the chairs are orderly and neat, are they not?'

'Yes, Khanum.' And without further instruction, the students giggled and got up to put the room in its familiar order.

After the children had gone for the day, Hasan and Ali helped Khanum put the finishing touches to the cleaning of the classroom. Hasan looked out over the now changed room and smiled to recall the morning game. It was more than a game. He had learned quite as much as the children. He had known the pleasure of watching minds awaken. He had been honoured to be their guide, even if it had been in mock seriousness.

Most of these children knew more about their religion than did he, but here among this simple community of believers he felt that learning, even for him, might be considered a joy, not a disease to be cured or a sin needful of atonement. But more than that, he sensed that from this simple exercise he had glimpsed more than a child's model of life's journey − he had become enamoured of a process, indeed of a profession, which could be as exciting and imaginative as it was noble in its aims. At that moment Hasan determined that some day he too would be a teacher of children.

6

The Word Made Flesh

FOR the next two weeks Ali and Hasan helped Maryam teach the young children. Each day when the classes were finished, the boys would drive the carriage back to the small cottage, though twice they walked the distance, some six or seven kilometres.

Maryam no longer seemed intimidating to Hasan. He now began to understand that what kept the children in awe was her inscrutable method — they could never predict what she would do next or what she might expect of them. It was this element of surprise that made her classes exciting.

But as Hasan observed these adventures in learning, he came to realize that this was not mere happenstance, not the benign accident of a spritely personality. Sometimes he arrived early enough to see her in the thick glasses that aided her failing eyesight. She would be labouring over tattered notes that might contain the outline of a game or project, for while her classes had the guise of spontaneity, she carefully planned them all.

One morning as he and Ali were getting the classroom in order, Hasan noticed her putting a small hammer in one of the deep pockets of the long dress she always wore.

'What are you going to do with that?' he asked.

'You'll find out soon enough,' she replied with a smile.

As the class progressed, she began discussing with them the relation-ship between the body and the soul. She took an old mirror and let them see in it a lighted candle which was otherwise concealed behind a screen. 'The candlelight is like the life of the soul,' she said, 'and the mirror is like the body. The mirror reflects the light, lets us see the qualities of the flame.' Then she spread a thin film of grease over the mirror. When she held up the mirror, the reflection of the candle flame was distorted and barely visible. 'When the mirror becomes clouded over, the qualities of the light are hard to observe, but is the light of the candle affected?'

'No,' said two students simultaneously. Maryam said nothing, but moved the screen aside, and indeed the candle flame was as bright and clear as before. She replaced the screen, and as she did so, she slid the small hammer from her pocket. With a quick short stroke she shattered the mirror. The pieces fell into a box she had placed beneath it, and the children gasped in shock.

'Now the mirror is gone,' she said. 'Does the light still shine?'

'How can we know?' said Jamal. 'You have broken the mirror.' Again Maryam moved the screen, and there the candle flame burned bright as ever. The children then discussed what they had seen, and they began to understand more about the subtle relationship between the spirit and the body.

Hasan was fascinated by the way Maryam had captured the imagin-ation of the children, but he was also intrigued by the analogy because it reminded him of Moayyed's description of the relationship between the moon and the sunlight. It started Hasan thinking again about his parents. Were they, like the candle's flame, still alive, still aware, still themselves in some placeless place?

That evening Hasan was again awakened from his sleep by a dream about his parents. As before, Moayyed heard Hasan stirring, moaning low in his sleep. The old man crept in the dark to the pallet where Hasan lay in a half sleep, and gently nudged him.

'Are you all right?' he asked.

'What?' said Hasan, rubbing his eyes. 'Oh, yes.' His yawn indicated he was. 'I saw Mother and Father,' he whispered. 'I saw Grandmother, too. I saw their faces.'

'Is that so?' said Moayyed.

'Yes, and they were smiling.'

'Good, good,' said Moayyed. 'Get some sleep, now. We leave early for Nuqayb.'

Nuqayb was a small village on the eastern shore of the Sea of Galilee, about thirteen kilometres from 'Adasíyyih. Just south of this village was a large tract of rich farmland which had been purchased by Bahá'u'lláh and settled by Bahá'u'lláh's faithful half-brother, Mírzá Muḥammad-Qulí, who had passed away not five years before.

The land was now occupied by his sons who, with the permission of 'Abdu'l-Bahá, had taken the name 'Bahá'í' when the Turkish government required everyone to take surnames. Moayyed was visiting the family partly to see old friends, and also to deliver instructions from 'Abdu'l-Bahá regarding the storing of grain to prepare for the inevitable hardship that would come as the war increased its burden on the people and food supplies grew scarce.

The carriage trundled its way along the shore road past occasional farms and small houses, as the sun was rising to their right from behind the heights of Golan. The water made a pleasant sound as it lapped the shore, and across the lake the colours of the hills of Galilee gradually changed hue as the sun ascended. The shadow of the Golan hills receded down the mountainside, though the lake itself was still untouched by sunlight, and a light mist hovered like steam above the smooth surface.

Before too long the warmth of the sun burned away the winter chill. The shadow was almost gone from the land, and the lake, like a giant mirror, reflected the village of Tiberias so perfectly that it was difficult to see where illusion ended and reality began. The sky changed from faint rose to golden yellow until the sun at last reached across the lake and shone on the carriage. Ali drove the wagon and listened as Moayyed described to Hasan the importance of this area.

'Two thousand years ago Christ taught his disciples along these very shores,' Moayyed explained.

Hasan listened intently. Raised as a Muslim, he knew about the

Prophets, believed that Christ was an Apostle of God, but he knew little about the intimate details of Christ's life and ministry. Then Moayyed motioned in a circle with his wrinkled hands. 'The Jordan River pumps water into this lake and the lake like a giant heart pumps that same nourishing water to the rest of this land, and the Holy Land itself is the source of life for the whole earth; it is the nest of the Prophets.'

'Sir,' said Hasan as he began to feel the special quality of this place and its sacred heritage, 'the other day when we were helping Maryam Khanum, we played a game. She called it the junkroom game.'

'The junkroom game. Ah, yes, she is becoming famous for it. You see, when some of the small children go home and begin to rearrange the furniture, parents wonder what is going on in Maryam's classes.'

'Well, I was the guide.'

'Yes?'

'Is that what Bahá'ís believe the Prophets are, guides?'

'Sometimes Bahá'u'lláh calls the Manifestations the Nightingales of Paradise because their voices call out in the darkness to remind us of the spiritual world, and with their teachings, their laws, the example of their lives, they guide us, true enough.'

'But in the game it all seemed so simple. One follows the guide and obtains rewards.'

'That is quite true.'

'But if it's so simple, why is there such confusion about religion. Why . . . why do people attack others in the name of religion?'

'Don't forget that before you can follow a guide you have to know who the guide is. And even then, even after you have discovered the true guide, you have to follow his guidance. Those two things aren't always so easy as you might think.'

'That's what I don't understand,' said Hasan. 'Why isn't it? If God wants everyone to recognize the Prophets and follow them, why don't they?'

'If you are asking why God's plan doesn't work, the answer is that it does, though it may not seem so if we draw our conclusions from observing a single moment in history.' He paused and looked out across the rich fields that rose up to the Golan. 'You see those fig trees? Now in the winter they are picked clean, pruned and bare. If you had to judge them, you would say they were not healthy, that they were not doing the job for which they were intended. But wait until they are laden with rich fruit and you will not be worried the next time you scc thcm in winter.'

'I would like to believe what you say, but if God's plan is working, why do even kings and rulers and men of great learning not understand it? Why don't they agree about what should be done? If I understand it, why can't they?'

'That's a very hard question to answer, Hasan. You see, there are different kinds of learning. Some things require only that we use our intellect, our reason. Other matters, like religious belief, require a quality of spirit, what I call a clarity of vision.'

'I don't understand.'

'I'm not sure I can explain it, Hasan. It has to do with putting aside the traditional responses to things. Christ told the learned Jews that they saw but they did not see, that they heard but did not hear.'

'What did He mean by that?'

'That they heard His words, but did not understand that He was fulfilling the teachings of Moses, that He was a Manifestation of God. For the most part it was the pure in heart, the unlearned who truly heard and saw, because this knowledge we are describing is available to everyone, to even the most unrefined of humankind. Bahá'u'lláh says that regardless of whether one is rich or poor, young or old, man or woman, a person of great learning or a simple peasant, all people have the ability to recognize the Manifestation when He appears and to follow His guidance. Only a few may be able to be scientists or great scholars, but everyone has the ability to understand spiritual qualities, to see goodness in another person, to appreciate these attributes.

'So it was that the simple fisherman could recognize and follow Christ, but the learned ones put Him to death. In the same way, the learned mullas were responsible for the death of the Báb and the cruel imprisonment of Bahá'u'lláh.' Moayyed did not go on to say the obvious — that these same religious leaders had probably been responsible for the death of Hasan's parents — it went without saying.

Moayyed motioned for Ali to stop the carriage and told him to water the horses. Hasan helped ease the old man down to the road because Moayyed's knees were bothering him more than usual.

'Let us rest for a while before we go on. It is only a few more kilometres, and I want to tell you both something about this family we are visiting. Besides,' Moayyed confessed, 'that carriage may be made of wood, but I am not, nor stone either. Ali, please get the cushion for me from the carriage.'

Ali retrieved the small pillow and Moayyed used it to make a place to sit on a large rock. Ali tended the horses, taking a tin to the lake shore to get them water, then he and Hasan sat down with Moayyed on the same boulder facing the water.

'Yes, it was across the lake along these very shores that Christ collected His disciples.'

'Like the Letters of the Living?' said Ali.

'Very much so,' said Moayyed. 'They were twelve instead of nineteen in number, but they were His faithful companions who spread the word of His teachings. However, Christ's disciples were not the learned, like Mullá Husayn, Quddús, or Ṭáhirih. They were simple fishermen like those you see casting their nets even now.' Hasan and Ali looked out at several small craft fishing far out on the water.

'Of course, the same is true today. The villagers in 'Adasíyyih are simple farmers, and yet they have discovered Bahá'u'lláh. You see how it is, Hasan? Who had more wisdom, the Jewish elders and leaders who were responsible for the martyrdom of Christ, or the simple fishermen who could not read or write but who became the first followers of the Prophet and spread His teachings throughout the known world? And who are the truly knowledgeable ones today, those simple farmers in 'Adasíyyih, or the rich and respected world leaders who are at this very moment ordering thousands of innocent people into battle to win more land for their own selfish desires?'

Normally Moayyed was calm and serene when he talked about

religion, but now his tone was strained, and the boys noted the stern aspect of his face, as if he would happily seize the misguided leaders, pick them up by their shoulders and shake them for their unwisdom.

Neither Hasan nor Ali spoke. They looked at each other in surprise. Moayyed became quiet, then smiled and squeezed Ali's arm.

'Forgive me,' he said. 'It is all well and good to talk about belief, but the suffering of mankind is hard to abide, most especially when it is perpetrated in the name of religion. In fact, the very first thing Bahá'u'lláh observes in *The Book of Certitude* is the irony that the very ones who say they await the promised messengers of God have throughout history so often been the ones who most fervently reject the new revelation and persecute the followers.

'But I do understand your question, Hasan,' Moayyed went on. 'What disturbs you is why God teaches us the way He does, why He conceals the promised guides. Why must they appear unexpectedly with strange names in strange places?'

'Yes, that's part of it,' said Hasan. 'When Maryam Khanum had me help the young children, she told them I would be their guide.'

'And God does not?'

'Does He?'

'Through prophecy He tells us, but also remember that the Prophets themselves say precisely who they are. They are not ashamed of their authority or their station. Bahá'u'lláh wrote letters to most of the world's religious and political leaders and told them exactly who He was and what they should do.'

'He did?'

'He certainly did. And when the Báb was being questioned by the government, He told them in no uncertain terms that He was the Promised Qá'im. But who listened?' He paused. 'Hasan, did the first student follow your advice every time?'

'No.'

'You see, Maryam let the students discover for themselves that it would be to their advantage to do what you said.'

'But why must it be so? Why does God allow us to choose? We might hurt ourselves by deciding incorrectly.'

'When you have a test in school,' said Ali, recalling an analogy he had learned from his father, 'what would happen if the teacher gave you all the answers beforehand?'

Hasan considered the proposition. At first the idea appealed to him, then he admitted that the test would not accomplish much.

'Why not?' asked Moayyed. 'In both cases you would have the answers.'

'Because I am supposed to be learning how to solve problems on my own, not just memorize answers.'

'It is the same with spiritual education,' said Moayyed. 'You are supposed to discover how to recognize spiritual qualities on your own, not simply memorize a name or a set of laws and prophecies.

'Let me explain what I mean with a true story that happened right here.' He pointed northward across the lake. 'Like all the Manifestations, Christ attracted people like a magnet. They always wanted to be with Him and listen to Him, just as the men flocked to see the Báb and Bahá'u'lláh. Sometimes they followed Him because they had heard He could heal the sick and do other things they considered miracles.'

'Could Bahá'u'lláh perform miracles?' asked Ali.

'The Manifestations have powers quite beyond anything we can understand,' said Moayyed, 'but they act in whatever way is best for teaching the people they come to. Christ performed miracles and so did the Báb and Bahá'u'lláh, but Bahá'u'lláh and 'Abdu'l-Bahá as well have cautioned us against placing too much emphasis on these phenomenal expressions of the Prophet's power.'

'Why?' asked Hasan. 'It seems to me that a miracle would be a good way to show people that the Manifestation is more than an ordinary man.'

'No doubt, at least for those who happen to witness them. The problem is, you see, that a miracle is not a sufficient basis for knowing who the Manifestation is or what His true nature is.'

'I don't understand,' said Hasan.

'For those who witness and believe, there is the problem of what it is they have faith in − the powers of the Manifestation to do fantastic things, or the spiritual teachings that these acts symbolize. The true value of these occurrences is the spiritual principles they symbolize. When Christ healed the sick, He was not trying to be a doctor or rid the land of disease, was He?'

'No,' said Hasan with a smile.

'Of course not. He was trying to show that the source of all health is the power of God revealed through the Manifestation. After all, many people can do things that seem miraculous, and people who see miracles may later question what they have experienced if all they understand or believe in is the capacity of the Manifestation to do physical things.

'But let me give you an example of what I mean, because it was here in this very land, after all, that so many of the miracles of the Prophets have taken place. Right over there, across the lake, one day Christ was teaching a group of people on the hillside. As usual the group got larger and larger. Hours passed and the day grew long. The people became hungry, but naturally no one had brought enough food for such a gathering. There were only a few dried fish and a few loaves which a young boy had brought.

'Christ commanded them to take these meagre morsels and feed all the people. Suddenly, there was enough food for everyone. No matter how much food they gave, there was always more than enough for the next person.' Moayyed paused and smiled as he watched the look of astonishment on Hasan's face.

'He did that right over there across the lake?' asked Hasan.

'Yes,' said Moayyed. 'But that's not the end of the story. When the people saw the miracle He performed, they immediately wanted to crown Him king.'

'Was He pleased?' asked Ali.

'Not at all,' said Moayyed. 'When Christ saw that they did not understand the spiritual significance of what He was doing, He withdrew by Himself to the hills.

'The next day the people found Him on the other side of the sea and they asked Him why He had left. He responded that they should not follow Him because He performed a physical miracle of producing food; they should follow Him because He could give them something much more important — '

'Spiritual food?' suggested Ali.

'Precisely,' said Moayyed. 'He had been trying to teach them a spiritual lesson, that God will provide for everyone, that there is no end to God's abundance. Christ went on to tell them that He was the spiritual nourishment sent to them by God − the "bread of life", a source of nourishment that would never be depleted.'

'Their guide?' asked Hasan.

'That's it,' said Moayyed.

'But how did He finally make it clear to them what He meant?' asked Hasan.

'That's the point,' said Moayyed. 'Only a few ever did understand. Three hundred years after Christ appeared, people were still debating who He was and what His teachings meant. Some believed He was the Messiah, but few understood exactly what that meant. Some believed He was a Prophet while others believed He was God.'

This notion shocked Hasan. 'How could they believe such a thing, that a man could be God?'

'They did not know how else to account for the things He could do and the spiritual power He possessed. He told them that everything He said and did was from God, not from Himself. He told them that when they studied Him and His teachings, they were really under-standing God working through Him. But because they had never known anything like Him, they attributed to Him the highest station they knew. And so three hundred years after Christ's death at a meeting in Nicaea, not far from Constantinople, the leaders of the Christian Church took a vote and decided that Christ was God.'

'How strange,' said Hasan.

'Yes, and how sad. By the time Muḥammad appeared − some three hundred years later, the Christian church was very confused in its understanding of Christ's teachings. In fact, in the Qur'án, Muḥammad addresses the Christians and makes a point of explaining that Christ was neither God nor the physical Son of God, but an Apostle of God, a Prophet, what Bahá'ís call a Manifestation. Like Bahá'u'lláh, Muḥammad explains that God has always sent such guides because all the religions of God are really one religion. It may be taught in stages. It may have different names and different teachers, but it is all the same religion.'

'Is that why the followers of Christ failed to become Muslims when Muḥammad appeared?' asked Ali.

'The followers of Moses persecuted the early Christians,' said Moayyed. 'The followers of Christ warred against the Muslims. Now the followers of Muḥammad persecute the Bahá'ís.'

Moayyed paused, looked up as if groping for just the right explanation. 'Let me put it this way, at least two problems have occurred. Some people become confused about what a Prophet is. They may think the Prophets are less than they are — simply good men or inspired leaders. This often happens with those who are very close to them and see only another human being who must eat and sleep, who gets ill and suffers as they do. But others may see them as more than they are, as God incarnate.'

'I guess it's not so simple after all,' said Hasan.

'It could be. It should be. The truth is simple, much more simple than falsehood. But this is what is so remarkable about the family we are going to visit. Mírzá Muḥammad-Qulí was one of the truly faithful members of Bahá'u'lláh's own family. Unlike Mírzá Yaḥyá, who tried to kill Bahá'u'lláh, Mírzá Muḥammad-Qulí was ever faithful and humble and loving. To him the truth was always simple and clear. His brother was a Manifestation and he regarded Him accordingly.

'Imagine it, though. Imagine how hard it might be to recognize a Manifestation if He were your own brother. It is one thing to read the words and teachings of a Prophet and decide that they are true. But your own brother? You would be tempted to wonder how someone born of the same parents and raised with you in the same household could be of such a high spiritual station. You might wonder why He should receive such high regard and not you.'

'It would be easy to be jealous,' observed Ali.

Hasan looked out across the lake at what might have been the very spot where Christ had fed the masses. Then he looked northward toward the shore, along which now lived the descendants of Mírzá Muḥammad-Qulí. A few gulls shrieked as they dived for minnows and their voices echoed. In a barely audible voice Hasan spoke to Moayyed. 'Sir, how does one become a Bahá'í?'

'One tries,' said Moayyed. 'That is all anyone can do. To take the name "Bahá'í" does not mean you have become something else. It is a sign of a goal you have chosen, a path for your soul.'

'Will you help me discover that path?' asked Hasan.

'We all will,' said Ali.

7

The Nightingale of Paradise

'BREATHE in,' said Dhikru'lláh, expanding his arms like a large awkward bird. 'The morning air is the best air.'

Hasan was too embarrassed to extend his arms, but he did inhale deeply, and the air was sweet and cool.

'Air is food for your blood, did you know that?' Dhikru'lláh continued as he walked. 'Did you learn that yet? You breathe in, the blood courses through tiny capillaries in your lungs, receives the life-giving oxygen, then your blood takes the oxygen along with other nutrients to all the parts of the body.'

'Yes, sir, I see what you mean,' said Hasan. 'I learned something about that.' Hasan tried to talk and keep pace with the athletic strides of the middle-aged man as they walked the rugged path from the level pasturage up the steep slope to the 'special place' that Dhikru'lláh had promised.

'Prayer is like that,' he continued. 'Food for the soul. No matter how sincerely you pray today, you will need to pray tomorrow.' He was a man in his forties, but he appeared much younger – the arduous hike did not even make him pause. 'You can't go more than a few minutes without air.'

'Yes, sir,' said Hasan, his voice hissing from trying to breathe and talk at the same time. He was not used to such a pace, and he was somewhat bemused by the offhand lecture.

'It is a blessing and a burden, you know, being called ''Bahá'í''.'

At first Hasan thought he was referring to being a Bahá'í, but then he realized that Dhikru'lláh was referring to the family name they had assumed.

'It's an honour, naturally, but I certainly have to watch everything I say and do. I suppose that's the wisdom in it, really.'

He stopped, not because he was tired, but to emphasize the thought, which he did by pointing his finger at Hasan, as if his observations were aimed specifically at the young boy's heart.

'Of course, all who follow Bahá'u'lláh bear the burden of the name ''Bahá'í'' ... *and* the honour of that title as well,' he added.

'Yes, sir,' said Hasan again, 'I'll remember.' For some reason Hasan was not the least offended by these axioms. He was sure that this youngest son of Mírzá Muḥammad-Qulí, this nephew of Bahá'u'lláh Himself, knew that Hasan was not a Bahá'í, but there was such sincerity, such real concern and tenderness beneath Dhikru'lláh's brusque exterior that Hasan could not help feeling great affection for this stranger at whose house he, Ali and Moayyed had received such a loving welcome.

The day before, a sudden rainstorm had caught them unprepared as the carriage neared Nuqayb, and they had sought shelter as best they could beneath the dilapidated roof of what had once been a small cottage. When they had finally reached the home of Dhikru'lláh and his family, they were cold and wet, but they had received a welcome fit for royalty — warm clothes, several large bowls of homemade soup, bread still warm from the baking oven and freshly-made cheese.

This house was more elaborate than the simple cottage where Hormoz lived. The Bahá'ís had comfortable furniture, several rooms for sleeping, and a number of beautiful artifacts from their native Persia. And yet there was a quality about this family that showed the same kindness and affection that Hasan had felt with Ali's family, with Hormoz, and with Maryam. He felt as if he were simply in another room of a very large household. All of them accepted him

without guile or pretence, and Hasan had the distinct impression it
was not because he was the son of Bahá'í martyrs — he felt in his
heart that they would have been just as gracious with a perfect
stranger.

It was after dinner that night when Dhikru'lláh had proposed the
morning walk. Hasan had been so bold as to remark how special it
must have been to be part of the family of a Manifestation of God.
Dhikru'lláh smiled brightly at the remark and announced, 'This
young boy deserves to visit my special place.' Later he made it clear
that this was to be a private thing between him and Hasan — no one
else was invited.

Soon they reached a small terrace on the hillside shaded by a few
scrub trees. It did not seem particularly special, but Dhikru'lláh assured Hasan that this was the place. He spread a small square of
canvas on the ground and motioned for Hasan to be seated.

Hasan looked out from several hundred feet up the Heights of
Golan at one of the most beautiful sights he had ever seen. The setting
was magnificent. It seemed for all the world like a painting by one of
the masters. The sky was laced with layers of grey and blue and rose-
fingered clouds. The water of the lake was placid, deep blue, not like
water at all from this perspective. The village of Tiberias was nestled
on the opposite side of the lake, and the mountains which rose up
behind Tiberias were just beginning to reflect in bright colours the
rays of the morning sun behind them.

'It will be some time before you can see the sun from here,' said
Dhikru'lláh, 'only its effects as it travels down the mountainside.'

'I saw the sun rise over the lake as we travelled here yesterday,' said
Hasan. 'It was beautiful, but nothing like *this*!'

Hasan wondered if this was how the world was before man evolved
on earth, when only a few creatures inhabited the fields and lakes.

'Like the Muslims, we face the Qiblih when we pray,' said
Dhikru'lláh, 'only instead of Mecca, the Qiblih for Bahá'ís is Bahjí,
the mansion outside 'Akká where Bahá'u'lláh is buried.'

He pointed almost directly across the lake toward 'Akká. Then he stood, folded his arms, and began to chant: 'I give praise to Thee, O my God, that Thou has awakened me out of my sleep, and brought me forth after my disappearance, and raised me up from my slumber. I have wakened this morning with my face set toward the splendours of the Daystar of Thy Revelation . . .'

Hasan stood too and listened to the words. When the prayer was over, Dhikru'lláh hesitated for a moment, then sat down. He looked out toward the Galilee mountains and said, 'Soon the sun will travel down the peaks to the water's edge.' Then without changing his tone or his look he asked, 'Have you ever been wakened by nightingales?'

'Yes, sir,' said Hasan.

'Beautiful bird, lovely voice. But when you are sleeping peacefully they can make a racket and you wish they would stop.'

'That's true,' said Hasan. 'I remember once staying at my uncle's house in Iṣfáhán. He had a beautiful garden, and the nightingales sang all night long. Uncle was used to it, but I wasn't and it kept me awake the whole night.'

'Bahá'u'lláh calls the Prophets nightingales – "Nightingales of Paradise". Know why?'

'Because their words are beautiful like the nightingale's song?' guessed Hasan.

'Perhaps. Or possibly because they sing in the night when everyone wants to sleep. In the teachings of the Prophets light is a symbol of truth, enlightenment and knowledge. Darkness is a symbol of ignorance. Likewise, being awake is a symbol of searching for the truth and being asleep is a symbol of heedlessness.'

'I see,' said Hasan.

'The Manifestation appears when people least expect it. Did you know that? Christ said the promised one would come like a thief in the night, when everyone was asleep and unprepared. It is the same with the nightingale. He sings out his beautiful melodies when we are least ready for them, when we are asleep and unprepared for such vibrant song.'

'I had not thought about it that way,' Hasan admitted.

'The prayer I just chanted was revealed by Bahá'u'lláh as a

morning prayer. It thanks God for having wakened us from the sleep of ignorance and for enabling us to recognize the Manifestation.'

'How did Bahá'u'lláh know that the people praying it would be "awake", as you put it.'

'Why else would they be praying the prayer?' Dhikru'lláh said with a smile as he looked at Hasan.

The two were then silent, watching the sun crawl down the slopes while the small settlements around the lake were quiet in the morning darkness. An occasional light was visible in the farmhouses as workers dressed and readied to go about their routine tasks.

'The Báb devoted the whole of His brief life to preparing people for the appearance of Bahá'u'lláh, for the dawn of this day. And when He instructed the Letters of the Living to go out and teach, He compared them to fires kindled on the mountain-top in the darkness of night.' Dhikru'lláh paused again and pointed toward some farmhouses along the shore. 'See how clearly we can see even the small simple lights in the dark? When there is darkness in the world, good deeds stand out like that, like beacons guiding lost souls.

'Bahá'u'lláh revealed the Tablet of the Proof for Shaykh Muḥammad Báqir, an infamous persecutor of many Bahá'ís whom Bahá'u'lláh called the Wolf. Bahá'u'lláh told him, "O Báqir! Rely not on thy glory, and thy power. Thou art even as the last traces of sunlight upon the mountain-top." I always think about that passage when I come here in the evening, how the day of Muḥammad's revelation has passed and a new day has dawned.

'But in the morning I seem to hear the voice of Bahá'u'lláh when He said, "Arise, and lift up your voices, that haply they that are fast asleep may be awakened." It sometimes makes me want to shout out the news of this Faith so loud that the whole earth would be awakened.'

'Why don't you?' Hasan suggested.

'And so I shall,' said Dhikru'lláh, his face grim, determined, 'and so shall we all.'

Dhikru'lláh's enthusiasm was infectious. Hasan did not fully understand everything he said and, not being a Bahá'í, he could not appreciate the reverence with which his host regarded these hills, and 'Akká in particular. Hasan respected the Bahá'ís and he was daily more comforted by their respect for him and their obvious appreciation for his peculiar circumstance — the progeny of Bahá'í martyrs and yet himself neither a Bahá'í nor knowing a great deal about Bahá'í beliefs.

Hasan did not exactly consider himself a Muslim by name, though he knew more of the Qur'án and of the Islamic faith than he did about Bahá'í beliefs. Out of respect for his grandmother when she was alive, he had studied Islam, had abided by Islamic law and tradition, but he was always aware of how his parents had died and was never fully comfortable with or convinced by his grandmother's halting explanation of how his parents had become 'influenced by the Bábís' and had thereby infuriated some of the more fanatical mullas in Yazd.

All the Bahá'ís he had ever seen or met in Yazd and now in Syria hardly seemed misguided or fanatical. And yet his grandmother's admonition made him cautious.

'Who do you think Bahá'u'lláh was?' asked Dhikru'lláh out of the blue.

'Sir?'

'Who do you think Bahá'u'lláh was?'

'I am not sure.'

'Do you know what Bahá'u'lláh claimed to be?'

'A Prophet, a Manifestation.'

'Exactly. Do you know what this means?'

'A little. A Prophet is a messenger from God, someone who is sent to tell us what to do. He's a guide,' he added, remembering Maryam's game.

'And yet He is more, more than we can understand completely. That was why it was indeed difficult for those in the family to understand completely the power Bahá'u'lláh had, the loftiness of His spiritual station. That's why your question touched me so last night. It was — it is — an incalculable honour to be a part of this family, and yet it is a test as well.'

Dhikru'lláh looked down toward the lake at a small flock of sheep dotting the pasture. 'If I were to dress you like a sheep, put you in a fleece, and have you crawl on all fours down there among my herd, would you be a sheep?'

'No!' laughed Hasan. 'Certainly not.'

'And yet the sheep might think you a sheep if you bleated exactly right and looked and smelled like a sheep.'

'I suppose so,' said Hasan, 'but I should not much enjoy crawling around with them, though I like sheep, especially the taste of them.'

'Neither does the Prophet enjoy his task of living among those who do not understand who or what a Prophet is. Why do you think they submit themselves to such indignities as being martyred on crosses or placed in dungeons?'

'You mean that the Prophets are not ordinary people?'

'Physically they appear to be so, but they are hardly ordinary. They have no need of learning or schooling, and when they reveal guidance, it is not as you or I might compose something, labouring over each sentence, each word. No, the words pour forth from the Prophets like water from a fountain, because God speaks through them, not indirectly as He might through you or me, but directly. He speaks to them. He tells them what to say. Can you imagine such a thing?

'That, my young man, is why it is so difficult for those around them during their lifetime to recognize who and what they are. Several of my own uncles plotted against Bahá'u'lláh because they saw only the physical man. He walked, He talked, He suffered, and yet people flocked to see Him from hundreds and thousands of miles away. Well, my uncles became jealous of that magnetic attraction and decided they would try to seize it for themselves. Think about that! They actually thought to steal that spiritual perfection, just as the sheep might envy you your knowledge if you started leading them around.

'But the power of Prophethood is not something you can seize or aspire to. A Manifestation is special from birth; He only seems to be another human being.'

'But why?' asked Hasan. 'I asked Moayyed only yesterday and he helped me understand it better, but I still don't understand why God must teach us so mysteriously.'

'Because it works. Because it is the best way to do what needs to be done. Do you think God is not wise? Then He would not be God, would He?'

Hasan looked down, thinking Dhikru'lláh was finished. He was discouraged. Then Dhikru'lláh continued.

'Let me give you an example of why His method works. Let us assume that I want to teach the children in the village of Nuqayb to play soccer, but they have never seen or heard of the game. And yet, because I want them to have a true love of the sport, I don't want to go to them as an adult and order them to play, even if I think that they might enjoy it.'

'Why not?'

'Because they might then think to themselves that they are playing only because I have made them, not because they find it fun to do.'

'So what do you do?'

'I will send you!'

'Dressed as a sheep again?' said Hasan, laughing.

'No, dressed as a village boy. However, I will have taught you all there is to know about soccer, and furthermore, I will tell you exactly what to say and do when you are among the village children. However, because I know those children well, I will not have you simply go in and say, "I am smarter than you and I know a game you will enjoy and I alone can teach you." No, no, that would instantly make them dislike you.'

'Very true,' said Hasan, remembering vividly the taunting of his classmates and the thoughtless cruelty that children can exhibit. 'Then how shall I teach them?'

'First, I will have you live among them awhile. Then I will have you pick out from among your compatriots those you find to be most capable of playing the game, those who would play well and who would enjoy sharing their new-found knowledge with others.'

'Good plan,' said Hasan.

'Then you will have them play a few games, inconspicuously at first. And as other children see them playing, see how healthy and happy they become, they too will desire to learn the game. And soon all the children will want to learn to play. And when they discover that you, Hasan, are the best source of knowledge of the game, they will come to you to discover the subtleties of the sport and what other games you might know.'

'And what shall I tell them?'

'If you told the truth, you would tell them you know only what I have taught you. You may tell them that you are only my representative whom I have sent to teach them the game. But since they cannot see me, they will praise you because they can see you and hear you.'

'And what do I do then?'

'You remind them that you are only the means by which they can learn the game.'

'And will they believe me? Will they understand?'

'Some may not, but many will. They will teach others and I will have accomplished my goal of teaching these children without actually going into the village myself and without imposing my will on them. And they will be the better for it because they will have chosen the game for themselves.'

'It would work, wouldn't it?' said Hasan.

'Indeed,' said Dhikru'lláh.

'But why must it take so long? Why must there be so many teachers over so many thousands of years, and yet still most of the village does not know how to "play the game", as you put it?'

'How long would it take you to teach the children to play soccer well?'

'A few days, I suppose.'

'To play *well*, I said.'

'A few weeks, months, perhaps,' said Hasan with a smile.

'Even if you tried as hard as you could?'

'Yes.'

'Even if they tried as hard as they could?'

'Yes.'

'And why is that?'

'Because they can learn only so many things at a time. I might be able to describe the rules to begin with. Then I would have to begin to teach them the particular skills they would need. Then they would need to practise.'

'And each day they would take what they learned the day before and build on that until they became more and more proficient in their skills?'

'Yes, exactly.'

'Look at the villages around the lake, Hasan; what do you see?'

'They are in the sunlight now.'

'And soon we will be as well, and we have found joy and peace in watching the sun rise and in feeling its warmth gradually change the cold night air into the warm and invigorating morning time. But what would happen if in the middle of the night the sun appeared in its full noontime potency and splendour.'

'It would be very shocking!' said Hasan.

'It would be devastating,' said Dhikru'lláh. 'Instead of this beautiful process of the sun's dawning, the sudden blast of light would utterly destroy us. We would all be blinded, and the pleasurable wakening would become a hideous nightmare. Listen to these words of Bahá'u'lláh: "Know of a certainty that in every Dispensation the light of Divine Revelation hath been vouchsafed unto men in direct proportion to their spiritual capacity. Consider the sun. How feeble its rays the moment it appeareth above the horizon. How gradually its warmth and potency increase as it approacheth its zenith, enabling meanwhile all created things to adapt themselves to the growing intensity of its light." He goes on to say, "Were it, all of a sudden, to manifest the energies latent within it, it would, no doubt, cause injury to all created things."'

'In other words, we can only develop so much at one time.'

'Correct. Growth of any sort must be gradual.'

Neither spoke for a while. Hasan considered Dhikru'lláh's words, then asked in a bemused tone a question to which he did not expect an answer.

'I wonder where it all began?' he said.

'It has no beginning. It will have no end.'

'None at all?'

'This planet may come into being and through the countless aeons of time change until it achieves the perfection that only the mind of God can envision. And it will go out of being when its time is done, hundreds of thousands of years from now. But creation itself continues without hindrance from the beginning which has no beginning until the end which has no end.'

'I never knew that.'

'How could it be otherwise? If God is the Creator and He is eternal, then He must have been creating eternally and He will never cease. Think of this planet as a cell in the body of the universe. It comes into being; it goes out of being. And in the course of its life it nourishes the universe just as it is nourished by it. This cell may be temporary, but the vast and endless body lives on as it always has.'

Hasan smiled, then looked out across the blue waters. His stomach grumbled and Dhikru'lláh observed that it was time for them to get their own nourishment.

As they walked back down the slope, Hasan studied this gentle man and wondered if he looked at all like his uncle Bahá'u'lláh. Then he wondered if he, Hasan, would have seen in that uncle merely another man, or if he might have been one of those able to penetrate the human surfaces to perceive the Manifestation within.

After they reached the level pasture, Hasan ventured another question, carefully phrased so as not to seem ungrateful or rude.

'Why is everyone so nice to me?' he asked.

Dhikru'lláh laughed heartily. 'What, do you think there is some conspiracy of goodwill, my boy?' He laughed some more, then said, 'I hope we are kind to everyone. But you are special to us, after all.'

'I, special?' asked Hasan.

'You are our legacy.'

'Why is that?'

'Your parents gave their lives that all of us, all the family of Bahá might bear this weighty title. Can we do less than serve in their place as they served in ours?'

'Then you knew who I was even before I came yesterday?'

'We did not know you were coming to our humble house, but we knew you had come to 'Akká.'

'How did you know?'

'We are presently a small community, a family of believers scattered in a few countries throughout the world, and the names of those who have paid the ultimate price for their beliefs, for our beliefs, are inscribed indelibly on our hearts just as they will be inscribed in the annals of history, as heroes of this age.'

'My parents — heroes?'

'You didn't know?'

Hasan said little on the way back to the house. He kept to himself the rest of the day, and the others respected his desire to be alone.

How much else had he not learned? he wondered. Heroes. His own parents were known throughout the world among the Bahá'ís. He would be patient, but he now determined that he would pursue this heritage. It was, after all, his birthright.

He no longer resented his grandmother's secrecy about the whole thing. He doubted that she had known with what esteem her daughter and son-in-law were regarded. Perhaps she had only desired that her grandson might be kept from the same fate. In any case, he thought, she knows now.

That evening he said a special prayer for the lady who had sheltered him. If she had kept him from the truth, it was with a pure motive.

'Motive is all,' she had told him. 'God will take care of the rest.'

She was right, he thought after his prayers, and somewhere she too is being consoled by this same verity.

8

A Mystery among His Mysteries

MOAYYED and the two boys stayed for several days in Nuqayb. And while Ali was helping Moayyed and Dhikru'lláh, Hasan assumed chores around the house, the most pleasurable of which, strange to say, was the care of an elderly aunt whom everyone addressed simply as Khanum. She was crippled, in her eighties, but respected by all as possessing the final insight concerning any problem.

Hasan enjoyed the life here, though he still felt somewhat of an outsider. He was a member of the family, but he was not a Bahá'í, and most of the family life centred around their activities as Bahá'ís. He did not feel they were fanatics — they were most open to him and not at all disdainful of those who were not of their Faith. But since Hasan himself was not a Bahá'í, he felt somewhat uncomfortable with their respect for the figure of Bahá'u'lláh. They did not worship Him, but Hasan, though having great regard for the logic and inclusiveness of their beliefs, found it difficult to think of this Persian exile who had died only twenty or so years before as having the same station, the same authority and esteem as timeless figures like Muḥammad and Christ, faceless names whose words and wisdom had transformed the world.

In his heart he wanted them to be right, wanted his parents to have given their lives for something enduring, something real and true. Therefore it was sometimes with dread that he asked questions or approached the Bahá'í scriptures, fearful lest he discover in them anything bizarre or illogical. But the more he searched without discovering a hint of anything offensive, the more relaxed he felt with these people, and the more eagerly he pursued his questions.

Hasan also began to notice something about himself that Moayyed and Ali had noticed as well. He was becoming less sombre. He smiled more than he frowned. He was gaining weight and becoming stronger so that his clothes hardly fitted him. His face assumed a deep olive complexion and his cheeks became rose-coloured and healthy-looking.

Khanum commented on it several times to Hasan as he helped her from room to room, for though he was finding great solace in walking through the fields or along the shore, he spent increasingly more time with Khanum. Physically she reminded Hasan of his grandmother before she had died — frail and bent from the weight of years and life's sorrows. But Khanum was cheerful, more cheerful than any healthy person Hasan had ever met, and he wondered why.

She leaned heavily on a cane when she walked, which was seldom. A chill would pass through Hasan when he watched her trying to manoeuvre from room to room — she could not disguise the pain then, and Hasan could see the knees tremble through the long dark dress and see the waves of anguish sweep the wrinkled face. He wondered why her legs, bent at acute angles from arthritis, did not simply break at the knees.

But when she talked or became lost in thought or became engrossed in the enchanting stories she told about the early days of the Faith in her village of Hamadán, Hasan forgot about her frail body. It was as if the years dropped from her face like gossamer veils. In those moments he saw in her eyes and smile a semblance of the young woman in the worn picture on the wall, standing proud beside her husband, whose bearded face and deep-set eyes betokened a regal dignity.

Sometimes she would talk about being old. She would speak as if her body belonged to someone else, as if it were her enemy, or else a ragged garment she was obliged to wear. She would talk about how lovely it might be to stroll once more in country fields. 'But this used-up shell of a body is too worn out,' she would say at last. 'I must drag it with me wherever I go.'

The idea teased Hasan's mind for several days, because while Khanum said such things in self-deprecating humour, it seemed so accurate to him. Khanum the woman, the personality, the spirit, seemed trapped inside a broken machine that would no longer do her will, that was indeed as alien to her as a tattered frock that no longer fitted.

The third night, as Hasan lay awake with this thought on his mind, he sat up in bed in the small room he shared with Ali. In the faint light that reflected from the waning moon he felt his own arm. It seemed as inseparable from him as his own thoughts. Why was it so different for her? What strange process could cause such a schism?

She was different from his grandmother, different really from all the old people he remembered in Yazd who sat blank-faced like discarded chairs and talked with a pathetic whine. Their spirits seemed as ragged as their frames. More than anyone Hasan had ever met or seen, Khanum seemed to be an incongruous mixture of essential youthfulness in an aged shell.

As he finally drifted off to sleep, Hasan wondered if he would ever look at his own arms and find them weak and wrinkled, if he too would some day find his body a nuisance, something that needed tending.

The next day everyone had work to do. Moayyed, Dhikru'lláh and Ali had gone to visit nearby farmers to consult on how to carry out the Master's wishes regarding the storehouses for grain in Nuqayb and 'Adasíyyih. The women of the household went about their countless tasks, and Hasan was again charged with caring for Khanum. Today the air was brisk and cool, and Khanum decided, against all advice from her two daughters, that she would sit outside in the garden at the back of the cottage where she could look out across the lake.

Hasan obliged her as best he could, nervous at first about touching her, then amazed to see how really light she was, how easy it was to help her. As Hasan brought her some tea and medicine, he marvelled that here was someone so utterly inferior to him in size and strength and yet so eloquent and wise that he was completely humbled by her vibrant spirit. Suddenly the word 'spirit' stuck in his mind. For the first time in his life he fully appreciated the supremacy of the human spirit over one's physical strength.

At her request they sat and talked. She knew that Hasan felt awkward helping her, and she tried to assuage his discomfort.

'Bahá'u'lláh often spoke of *detachment* — you know what the word means?'

'Not really,' Hasan admitted.

'It means being *in* the world but not *of* the world. It means enjoying the things of this life, benefiting from them without becoming dependent on how much you possess or how you feel physically.'

'I see,' said Hasan politely, though he was not really sure what she meant.

'You know why this virtue is so important?'

'No, Khanum.'

'Because no *body* leaves this life alive.'

Hasan laughed. 'That's true, isn't it?'

'Don't you dare feel sorry for me, my young friend. Do you think you will not get old? It is part of God's wisdom. Most trees and many beasts live longer than we do. Animals are swifter, stronger. I sometimes wonder when I read about the war if animals aren't wiser. But you see, we are devised so marvellously well for our training — that's the point. As we get older, we also get wiser, provided we make an effort to do so. And because we are being prepared for the next world, God has designed our bodies so that they slowly but surely disintegrate right before our eyes.'

'Why is that good?' asked Hasan.

'Because it forces us to rely on our mind and spirit instead of on our physical abilities, because it prepares us for the inevitable transition to a life where physical bodies are no longer relevant. Of course, some stalwart souls are always ready, but for those of us who need extra encouragement, we are chased from this realm by an army of ills, as if they were saying, "Leave, Khanum, you have taken quite enough time to learn what you need to know."

'That's what I called "forced detachment",' she said with a high-pitched laugh. 'For those of us who have grown old without growing wise, who still believe we have a lot to learn, God finally makes this life so difficult that we gladly greet our birth into the next life, like a child who has overstayed its welcome in its mother's womb.'

Hasan laughed, then unconsciously felt his arm as he had the night before. He did not feel 'detached', as she put it. The arm was his, was him, Hasan − how could it be otherwise?

Suddenly he felt something prickly on his shoulder, as if someone from behind had put a hand upon him, only it wasn't like a hand. He sensed something beside his cheek softly nudging his ear. Instinctively he remained quite still and did not turn or jerk, and saw a look of sheer pleasure on Khanum's face.

'Careful,' she whispered.

Hasan remained still, as if it were a deadly spider on his shoulder instead of a small sparrow. Then, as if it were the most ordinary thing in the world, the bird casually hopped onto Hasan's arm. He was still motionless, certain the creature did not fully appreciate where it was.

The small brown-and-grey-flecked songster was no bigger than Hasan's hand. She cocked her head to look at Hasan's eyes, then nonchalantly preened, sang a note or two, and flew away. Hasan could feel the fluttering of wings like angels' breath in his ear as the small bird winged past him. Goose bumps travelled his arms. Hair stood on the back of his neck, and he giggled.

Khanum smiled benignly. 'That is Tela,' she said. 'We named her for the sound she makes. We fed her one morning several months ago and she keeps returning every so often to partake of our generosity.'

'Tela,' repeated Hasan, listening to the sound of the name. 'Will she always perch on your arm?'

'She's never done that before,' said Khanum.

Hasan was thrilled − such an honour to be chosen by this ephemeral creature, as if a spirit from another world had designated him alone to be the recipient of a special blessing.

Hasan and Khanum contined to talk for awhile, though Hasan's thoughts were of the bird. Try as he might to look at Khanum, he constantly scanned the trees and sky for a sign of the small sparrow.

Later that afternoon when no one else was around and Khanum was taking her nap, Hasan went into the garden alone and sat in the same chair and waited, very still. He so hoped the bird would return, as if to prove that he was graced with a special virtue that the wise little sparrow could perceive.

He became discouraged after several minutes passed and Tela did not come. He then took a handful of millet he had got from the kitchen and held his hand palm up so that his arm was a perch and his hand a feeding dish. The afternoon sun shone on his face in a lacy pattern as it filtered through the trees, and the breeze made the pattern trace back and forth across his eyes in such a hypnotic motion that soon he drifted into a light sleep.

He was wakened minutes later by the sense of something on his arm. Slowly, carefully, he opened his eyes to see Tela sitting there. He blinked his eyes once to be sure he was awake, but quickly the bird resolved all doubts by shuffling down his arm out to his hand. Unafraid, the bird perched on his thumb and pecked at the seed.

Hasan wanted so to close his hand, to hold the bird, to stroke its soft feathers. Instead he contented himself with watching her. He held his hand as steady as he was able, but soon his hand began to tremble. The bird pecked some more seed, paused, looked up, blinked, cocked its head as if it knew Hasan intimately. Then it turned, chirped once, as if it were giving a quick 'thanks', and flew away.

Hasan was amazed. Such delicate life and yet so wise and confident. Hasan had never known the wild. He had been a sickly child and given instead to reading and study. Neither did he ever have a pet, so he was all the more affected by this small miracle of a sparrow, the slight weight of those tiny feet on his wrist and hand, the expression he read into the cocked head and blinking eyes.

Tela did not return again that day, but Hasan took great pleasure in telling Khanum about feeding the bird. He left out no detail about how she had crawled up his arm and eaten, and especially how she had thanked him. Khanum nodded her head and smiled, 'Yes, birds are marvellous creatures, one of the Almighty's best designs.'

The next day Hasan begged to be excused from accompanying Ali and Moayyed to inspect the properties with Dhikru'lláh. Then, as soon as he could politely excuse himself from other duties, he went out back to the garden and sat in the wooden chair, his hand packed with seed. Three times the bird ate from his hand that day. When Tela wasn't eating from his hand, Hasan often saw her fluttering about the yard.

That evening as he lay in bed, the idea of a small bird eating from his hand was not so astounding to him as it had been the day before. But it was still special, and he woke the next morning looking forward to another series of encounters with his newly-discovered friend.

After breakfast he sat in the same spot, but no Tela. He waited for almost an hour, but still Tela did not appear. He saw several small birds darting among the trees. Each one seemed at first to be her, but none came to him.

It occurred to him that he might be doing something wrong. Possibly he looked different, was holding his hand wrong. He shifted the seed to the left hand, but nothing happened. He gave the chair a quarter turn, but no Tela. For almost two hours he waited, the seed now moist and crumbly in his warm hand.

At last he became utterly discouraged and went inside to help with chores in order to take his mind off his disappointment. Perhaps later Tela would get hungry and he would have more success, though in the back of his mind he knew that Tela had managed to live quite well before he had come to visit Nuqayb.

Several times during the day he went out into the yard and waited, but Tela did not come. He asked Khanum if she had seen the bird.

'No,' she said, 'but I did see Omar, and that does not bode well for our tiny friend.'

Omar, she explained, was a neighbouring cat that often roamed the garden looking for tasty morsels.

'Tela is too quick,' said Hasan. 'Besides, she can fly!'

'Omar is quick too,' said Khanum, 'and quite the crafty bird catcher.'

Hasan politely excused himself and immediately went out into the garden in a panic. He searched among the dormant roses and the evergreens that even winter could not stifle, but he saw nothing. Suddenly, as he searched around the grape arbour, a bushy golden cat jumped from the leaves. It was Omar and he was toying with a small bird!

'No!' Hasan screamed at the startled cat. 'Leave her alone!' Hasan sprang toward the cat, but the agile beast leaped away, snatching its prey just in time to avoid Hasan's grasp. Hasan chased behind as fast as he could and managed to make the frightened cat drop the mangled bird from its mouth as it sprang over a rock wall that bordered the garden.

His heart pounding with hope, Hasan retrieved the warm but lifeless sparrow. Its eyes were open, but its head drooped to one side. Hasan cupped the soft bird in his hand, quickly rubbed its breast, as if the tenderness of his touch could reverse the irresistible forces of nature.

Tears streamed down Hasan's face and blurred his vision of the lifeless form. Such innocence, such pure, untainted and delicate innocence wasted without reason. The tears gave way to deep sobs. His chest heaved uncontrollably as if all the untapped pain he had ever known came pouring through him, and he dropped to his knees.

How long he remained there he did not know, but after a while the tear flood ceased. His eyes were sticky from crying and he wiped them with the cuff of his coat sleeve. Slowly he got up and walked toward the house, the bird still in his hand. At the back doorway was Khanum who had seen it all.

'It's Tela,' said Hasan, his voice still hoarse from sorrow as he held forth the remnant of the once vibrant life. 'Omar killed her!'

Khanum consoled Hasan as best she could, then led him out to a small plot behind the garden where the two of them observed a solemn rite. Hasan gently laid the feathery corpse in the winter earth, and they said a prayer. Khanum remarked that Tela could now nourish the flowers she loved so well.

Hasan thought about these words as he helped Khanum to her favourite chair in the middle of the garden. After they were seated, Hasan asked, 'Don't birds and animals go on to the next world?'

'I think not,' said Khanum calmly.

'But why?' asked Hasan, with a slight hint of indignation.

'They don't need to,' said Khanum.

'But that's not fair,' said Hasan.

'The animals don't seem to mind it,' said Khanum.

'Because they don't know any better — is that what you mean?'

'That's the point, you see? Listen, Hasan, I know you are grief-stricken for the loss of your little friend, and that is proper; that is as it should be. She taught you something — about the mystery of tenderness, about kindness — but she is beyond feeling or suffering. She can hardly miss going to a world which she could not appreciate anyway.'

It was clear from Hasan's expression that he was not convinced or consoled, so Khanum continued. 'See the rosebush there? It seems quite dead now. It is leafless; its stems are trimmed back. It hardly seems like a flower. But in a few months, this garden will be fragrant with perfume from the blooms of those same drab stems. Each flower on the rosebush will live only a short time, a few days, no more. But the blooms don't mind. Each bud will glory in its purpose.'

'And what is that?' asked Hasan.

'To fill our lives with beauty and thereby remind us of the divine wisdom that created such marvels, to portray for us the laws of nature by which all of us are governed.'

'What laws are you talking about?'

'The cycles of life, for one thing. There is a fine wisdom in it — life and death, winter and spring, being born and dying. I do not mean to belittle your sorrow, Hasan,' said Khanum, patting his hand, 'though I suspect you were grieving for more than a lost sparrow. But the ruby does not begrudge the rose its fragrance. The rose does not envy the bird its flight, and Tela does not envy you your soul. Each thing in creation has its special way of sharing with us some quality of its Maker. It is up to you to listen for those messages, to learn from them and, having learned, change your life in ways that a rose or a sparrow is not meant to do. That is how you can bloom and give your own special qualities to the world of creation.'

'But Tela was so sweet and good,' said Hasan, still unconvinced. 'What am I to learn — that wicked cats should be allowed to kill defenceless birds?'

'Is Omar wicked for wanting to eat? What about Tela, eating defenceless worms?'

'But who cares about worms?' said Hasan.

'Other worms,' said Khanum, with a smile.

'You know what I mean,' said Hasan.

'Yes,' said Khanum. 'Yes, I do. Look, God has created us for one purpose, to know and to worship Him by discovering His qualities and by trying to make those same qualities part of our own nature. This is our only purpose in this life. This is the way we bloom, by becoming godly. According to all the Prophets, the purpose of nature and all its creatures is to help us in this noble and lofty goal.'

'You mean that nature and everything in it exists just to help us?'

'To help us spiritually, not physically. We do not own nature. We're not supposed to use it up or destroy it any more than I would give you a typewriter to help you learn to write and expect you to mutilate it.'

'How do you know it's not the other way around?' asked Hasan. 'Why are we so special? Tela was nicer than a lot of people I know.'

'Just because human beings are created with a special ability does not mean that everyone will use that capacity, does it? Humanity is the fruit of creation as the bloom is the fruit of the rosebush. It is so because human beings are uniquely capable of determining what they will become. Does the bush determine whether or not it will give forth flowers? Of course not. Only people can decide what will be the fruit of their lives. And there is a great danger in that power.'

'What danger?'

'We are capable of the greatest good but we are also capable of the greatest evil.'

Hasan looked over toward the small grave and remembered how

only the day before Tela had fluttered among the branches and lit on his arm like a fairy spirit.

'What makes us different?' he asked. 'Animals talk, in their own way. They walk, they sing. They can be good or bad.'

'To you Omar is bad because he took away your friend, but Omar only follows his instincts and training just as Tela did. From Tela's point of view, you provided food. Had you provided Omar food, that furry cat might have proved just as good a friend to you. With enough to eat, he might have decided not to attack Tela.'

'You mean there is no such thing as a bad animal?'

'There may be animals that are dangerous or that are untrustworthy because they have a disorder or a disease, but you cannot use human standards to judge an animal.'

'Can't they think?'

'After a fashion, some of them more profoundly than others.'

'But when you see a mother sheep nursing her lamb, don't you say that she is a good mother?'

'We may indeed say such things, but the fact is she is a good mother because it is her nature. She does not lie awake at night wondering if she has done well with her lamb or trying to determine how she might be a better parent.'

'But animals show affection and love.'

'Animals respond to kindness and we can learn incredible things from caring for them and observing them — how beings are affected by kindness, how learning takes place. As a child we may learn the fundamentals of responsibility and selflessness. Just because animals do not have souls does not mean they are without feeling or importance. No, just because they cannot consider moral questions does not mean they do not have a significant role in this world.'

Hasan listened carefully to Khanum's wisdom, then looked once more through the branches of the trees. 'It is all very hard to understand,' he said.

'That's why you have a lifetime to figure it out,' said Khanum, 'or at least to get started.'

Suddenly a small bird flew between them and startled them both.

Quickly it made another pass, then lit on Hasan's arm.

'It's Tela,' he said excitedly, and the frightened bird flew away.

'I guess that one sparrow looks pretty much like another,' said Khanum as she laughed.

'There is only one Tela!' said the delighted young boy, and he ran into the house to grab a handful of seed.

9

A Freedom of the Will

THE day after Tela returned, Hasan spent a good deal of time alone in his thoughts, walking by the shore of the lake along tranquil paths that gave no hint of the conflict in the world at large.

In Hasan's life something very positive was happening, part of which he understood, most of which he did not. He knew he was becoming stronger, emotionally as well as physically. The constant exercise, the fresh air of the countryside, and the fine meals were all having a dramatic effect on his appearance, and whatever was going on inside him made him feel at once serene and sturdy. Life no longer seemed a matter of endurance; he relished each day.

He thought about all this as he picked up some small rocks and skipped them across the water. It was a hard thing to describe, even to himself, but he felt as though he was now really Hasan, as if the sullen boy he had been was now a stranger to him. Unconsciously he rubbed his stomach, recalling the knotted feeling inside, the constant tightness. It too was fading. He had grown so used to such feelings that only their demise made him aware that they had existed.

During this same thoughtful walk Hasan determined for the first time that he truly wanted to be a Bahá'í. It was a decision based not on the tenets of the religion, logical and appealing as they seemed.

No, it was the Bahá'ís themselves who had impressed him, their willingness to talk with a thirteen-year-old boy when they had jobs to do and other people to care about. It was their respect for him, as if his ideas and questions were as valid and important as those of learned and lofty scholars.

His experience with the Bahá'ís might not have been so remarkable to him had he sensed this acceptance from only one or two people, or if he had detected any ulterior motive in their kindness. But he had become convinced that this was simply the nature of the Bahá'í community itself as it followed the guidance of Bahá'u'lláh. Somehow the Bahá'ís managed to maintain the thoroughness of their conviction without becoming narrow, fanatical or chauvinistic.

When he returned from his walk about an hour or so later, he decided to tell Khanum of his decision. 'I know I have much to learn before I am ready to call myself a Bahá'í,' he said, 'but I would like to try.'

Khanum reached up from her reading chair and gave him a heartfelt hug. She promised him she would always keep him in her thoughts and prayers, a simple assurance that Hasan was to recall often in years to come when he would feel her spirit guiding him. Then she cautioned him.

'Becoming a Bahá'í is not like magic. Do not think you have to wait until you have reached a certain level of perfection before you are worthy to grace yourself with so lofty a title – God forbid such a thing. The Almighty has bestowed the gift of this Faith on humanity as a tool for growth and advancement, not merely as a reward for those who are already perfected.'

The words comforted Hasan, but he still confessed to her that he yet had much to learn.

'You will know when you are ready,' she said. 'Only you will know.'

'Yes, Khanum,' he agreed. 'I think I will.'

'Then my gift is a timely one indeed,' said Khanum, reaching into a knitting bag where she kept a hundred and one things known only to her. She pulled out a small but beautifully penned copy of *The*

Hidden Words of Bahá'ulláh. She took the book to her lips with both hands as a sign of reverence, then handed it to Hasan.

He was overwhelmed with her kindness.

'But why?' he asked. 'I cannot accept so exquisite a gift!' He attempted to give it back, only to have her hold up her hands in protest.

'It is time for you to read, don't you see? Almost all you know about this Faith is through the description of others. That is all well and good in the beginning, to hear everything described simply and clearly by someone whose life has been touched by this Revelation. But if this Faith is to be yours — truly yours — if your beliefs are to be your own and not merely an imitation of someone else's belief, then you must go to the source of this religion.'

'The source?'

'Bahá'u'lláh,' Khanum replied. 'It is fine to learn about the Faith from Bahá'ís. After all, if they are not changed by their beliefs, then how important could this religion be? But after all, everything we believe is based on the teachings of Bahá'u'lláh. We didn't invent this Faith. It all derives from His pen. Therefore, it is time for you to turn to that source, because if your belief is to be firmly grounded, if you are to have the unshakable conviction your parents had, you must be sure your understanding is based on your own investigation of the writings of Bahá'u'lláh, not on what someone else tells you they say.'

Hasan accepted Khanum's advice as a challenge and a solace because he loved nothing more than reading and studying. He looked at the book and traced the embossed calligraphy with his fingertips.

'One thing more,' said Khanum.

'Yes?'

'Try to remember when you open the books of Bahá'u'lláh that the words are not His words — God is speaking to you through His Prophet. Therefore, each time you read the sacred texts, do so with a special reverence. Say to yourself, "God is about to speak to me. God is about to give me unfailing guidance for my life."'

Hasan never did forget her exhortation. For the rest of his life whenever he read from the revealed writings of Bahá'u'lláh, he remembered her advice and said a brief prayer for her.

As soon as he could find time alone that evening, he began to read the jewel-like utterances of *The Hidden Words*. Intended as a distillation of the essential spiritual truth of all the previous religions, each passage, each Hidden Word, was for Hasan an exquisite poem. Each verse was complete unto itself, each a mandate for humanity, and yet each Hidden Word flowed into and out of the other passages weaving a tapestry of enlightenment.

In the Persian section Hasan read: 'The first call of the Beloved is this: O mystic nightingale! Abide not but in the rose-garden of the spirit.' He thought about Dhikru'lláh's discussion of the symbolism of the nightingale. Then in the section which had been translated from the Arabic, he read: 'My first counsel is this: Possess a pure, kindly and radiant heart, that thine may be a sovereignty ancient, imperishable and everlasting.'

He did not understand every word, but the sound of the words was like music, and he felt himself deeply affected by the sense of each passage. The words themselves seemed to have a power beyond any exact meaning they might have. 'I loved thy creation, hence I created thee.' How simple; how clear. Like a parent wishing to share its love, God had created humankind that He might share that love. 'Wherefore, do thou love Me, that I may name thy name and fill thy soul with the spirit of life.'

He stopped at the next passage and could go no further. 'O Son of Being!' it began, 'Love Me, that I may love thee. If thou lovest Me not, My love can in no wise reach thee. Know this, O servant.' Suddenly instead of being comforted, he felt bewildered and confused. On the surface the meaning seemed clear enough – God cannot love us unless we love Him first. But the very idea felt alien to everything Hasan had come to believe about God.

He read it several times and his perplexity only increased. If God could do whatever He wanted, why was His love dependent on man's love? 'What about people who don't even know about God?' he mused. 'Are they to be deprived of God's love?' In particular he wondered about remote tribes in far-off jungles who might worship idols, creations of their own invention and imagination. How could a just God not extend His love to those not yet privileged to know and understand?

Hasan slept poorly that night because his mind could not let go of this paradox, and the question continued to run through his mind until the sky began to lighten. At last, out of sheer exhaustion, he let go of the thought and slept for a few hours.

When morning came, the enigmatic passage still haunted him so much that he was unable to go any further. Until he was satisfied in his own mind that God was fair and kind, how could he read any other passages with enthusiasm? As he and Ali were getting dressed, he mentioned the matter in an offhand way so as to hide the quiet desperation he actually felt.

At first Ali did not respond. He was so delighted to learn that Hasan wanted to be a Bahá'í that everything else seemed secondary.

'That's wonderful! But when did you decide this?' asked Ali.

'Yesterday,' said Hasan with a radiant smile.

'You are lucky, you know.'

'Why do you say that?' asked Hasan.

'Because you have come to your beliefs on your own. It's your personal discovery. You will never have to wonder if you are following what you believe, or simply doing what you were expected to do.'

'Is that what you did?' asked Hasan, astonished that anyone should envy him anything.

'No, my parents saw to that. Besides, I've always been too curious and stubborn.'

'It's funny you should think I am lucky,' said Hasan, 'because I envy you.'

'Why is that?'

'Because of your parents — because they raised you to know about your beliefs. It will take me years to learn what you already know.'

'I guess there are advantages both ways,' said Ali. 'I suppose in the long run we either make beliefs our own or else they aren't really ours, only a copy of what someone else believes.'

Ali's words surprised Hasan because they were so similar to what

Khanum had said. 'You haven't talked to Khanum about this, have you?' asked Hasan.

'No, why?'

'Just wondering. But look, what about my question – you never answered it.'

'Sorry,' said Ali. 'I forgot. Let's see, I think I know *what* the passage means, but I'm not sure I can put it into words, and I don't think I can tell you *how* it means.'

'What?'

'It has to do with choice,' said Ali, 'what Moayyed calls "freedom of the will". I think it means that everybody is free to decide whether or not they will love God.'

'But not everyone even *knows* about God,' said Hasan.

'That's true, isn't it. Well, I do remember one time Father talking about the same sort of thing. We were out in my boat at the time. There was no wind that day, at least not after we got out past the sea wall. Very unusual. Well, I was at the tiller and Father was simply relaxing for a change – something he almost never gets a chance to do. He was looking up at the sail hanging there useless on the mast. He looked at me sitting at the tiller. I was trying to look very knowledgeable and impressive so I fiddled with a rope, adjusted a cleat. I moved the boom, but of course nothing had any effect without wind.

'I was quite prepared for him to make a joke about the whole thing, but he was thinking about something else. Out of the blue he said to me, "God is like the wind and your soul is like that rudder", or something like that.

'I remember that at the time I did not have the slightest idea what he was talking about and told him so. He said that he had heard 'Abdu'l-Bahá use the same analogy to explain the meaning of "free will" and in the boat he could appreciate it. You see, according to the analogy, there is no life without God's creative force, no motion of any sort.'

'Like a sailboat without wind?' suggested Hasan.

'Right. Exactly. But when the winds come and there is motion, we must then use our free will to decide which way we will sail.'

'So our souls are like rudders, deciding which way we will go?'

'That's the way I understand it. Anyway, as we were talking Father quoted that same passage from *The Hidden Words*.'

'But doesn't it seem to you unfair that God will not love us unless we love Him first? I mean, if you decided you no longer loved your mother or father, do you think they would stop loving you?'

Ali paused as he was lacing his shoes. It was a hard question. He could not think of a good answer, and he suggested they ask Moayyed later.

Hasan tried to be polite and allow the adults to dominate the conversation at breakfast, but at last he could hold back no longer.

'Sir,' he said meekly to Moayyed, 'did you not tell me that God is independent, that He doesn't really *need* anything?'

'Perhaps I did,' said Moayyed, sipping his tea. 'In any case, it's certainly true enough. Why do you ask?'

'And did you not also tell me that God's love and bounties are available to all, even the sinful and the faithless?'

'I recall saying something like that.'

'God even sends the Prophets in spite of the fact that the people of the earth reject them.'

'Quite so, quite so,' said Moayyed.

'Why then does the Hidden Word say that God will not love us unless we love Him first? If He doesn't need our love, why would He care? And if He is merciful as you say, why would He not love us anyway?'

It was a subtle question and Moayyed set down his cup in astonishment.

'What's this all about?' he said with a bemused expression. 'A few days ago I brought a simple lad to visit, and suddenly he's Mírzá Abu'l-Faḍl incarnate!'

'He's decided to become a Bahá'í,' said Khanum with a knowing grin.

'So the irresistible charm of your spirit has captivated him, has it?' said Moayyed to Khanum affectionately.

'My, no,' said Khanum. 'I knew nothing about this until he told me.'

Everyone at the table expressed their joy in Hasan's decision, especially <u>Dh</u>ikru'lláh. But Moayyed interrupted the festivities by observing that no one had answered the boy's question. Ali mentioned the analogy of the sailboat, and Moayyed responded. 'Good! That's an excellent explanation. Perhaps we can come up with a few others that will explain the passage more directly.'

The old man sat back and stared briefly at the ceiling, as if he were opening his mind to receive divine insight. Soon he looked back across the table at Hasan. 'Have you ever been in a house with electric lights?'

'Yes, sir. Once.'

'And just how did you get light in that house?'

'There was a switch on the wall. One simply turns the switch and the lights come on.'

'So all that you need to have light in such a house is what?'

'I don't understand,' said Hasan.

'Nor I,' Ali rejoined.

'All right, all right. You go into the house, correct?'

They agreed.

'What do you need to get light in the house.'

'Before you turn the switch?' asked Ali.

'Yes, exactly.'

'Knowledge,' said Hasan. 'You have to know where the switch is and what it does.'

'Excellent,' said Moayyed. 'Quite so, quite so.' The others listened intently, because not even Khanum or <u>Dh</u>ikru'lláh had the slightest idea what point Moayyed was making. 'And even before your knowledge exists, there must be the system itself, do you understand? You may know all about the power of electricity and how the switches work, but without the miraculous power of electricity pulsing through those wires from the source of that power your knowledge would matter little.'

'But how does that explain the passage?' asked Hasan.

'Because Bahá'u'lláh and all the Prophets not only tell us about the system and explain where the switches are, they also assure us that the electricity is always there. God's power to assist us is ceaselessly flowing through the lines.'

Moayyed paused, took a sip of tea, then leaned back. 'But there is something we must do to receive that power, you see?'

'We must know where the switches are and how to turn them on?' suggested Ali.

'That and one thing more,' said Moayyed. 'You must do it. You must act. Because in the midst of darkness, even such marvellous technology cannot help you if you do not turn the switches.'

'But I still do not understand,' said Hasan, pointing his finger at the small book that he had brought with him to the table. 'It says here that God will not love us unless we love Him first. It seems to me that if God did not already love us, He would not have revealed where the "switches" are. Or for that matter, if God did not already love us, why would He have provided us with such a system?'

'Read the passage again,' said Moayyed.

Hasan opened the book to the passage and read: 'Love Me, that I may love thee. If thou lovest Me not, My love can in no wise reach thee. Know this, O servant.'

'Does the passage actually say that God will not love us unless we love Him first?'

Hasan scrutinized the words carefully, then read softly, '"My love can in no wise reach thee." *Reach* thee! *Reach* thee! That's the key, isn't it?' he said enthusiastically. 'God's love, like the electricity, is always there, but if we do not know about it and do not choose to respond to it, God will not force it upon us.'

'Because He cannot,' said Khanum. 'By its very nature love cannot be forced, cannot be imposed against the will because then it is no longer love. More than one parent has had to face that reality.'

'Just so,' said Moayyed.

'But why must we love God *first*,' asked Hasan. 'If He loves us like a parent, why would He wait for us to turn the switch, as you put it. Why must His love be dependent on ours?'

'You think He waits?' said Moayyed. 'No, no. By no means does He wait. It is we who deny Him access to our hearts. Let me explain.

Do you believe your grandmother loved you?'

'Yes, sir.'

'And your parents before her?'

Hasan lowered his eyes. 'Yes,' he said in barely audible tones. Then he looked up, his eyes clear and calm, and he spoke again, this time with certitude and conviction. 'Yes, sir.'

'And do you believe that we here at this table love you?'

'I think so,' he said with an embarrassed smile.

'And if you suddenly decided you no longer cared for us, do you honestly in your heart of hearts believe we would stop caring for you?'

Hasan did not respond instantly. He knew the answer, but the thought, though obvious to everyone, suddenly struck him as very profound and reassuring. No, he thought, they would not stop loving me — how remarkable that this affection, given so freely without pretext, was something he could always depend on. Suddenly he understood Moayyed's point before the older man spoke.

'Then can you believe that God, in whose love we were all created, who like a loving father has nurtured and guided His creation from the very beginning, would ever wait for our love before He gave His own? Surely the lives of each and every Manifestation, given so sacrificially by the Father, demonstrate the opposite.' He leaned forward as his voice became more intense. 'Think of the passage in the New Testament where John states that "God so loved the world, that he gave his only begotten Son". Would God allow His own Prophets to be so mistreated if He were not willing to give love without thought of return? No, my son. God's love may not be able to reach us unless we choose to receive it, but the love is always there, always waiting for us to receive it.'

There was silence for awhile as all around the table considered Moayyed's words as well as the astute mind of this bright youth. They were joyful in Hasan's joy and were astounded at his blossoming forth like a flower too long held tightly in the bud.

Hasan looked up, his face a mask of contentment. He closed the book and once again ran his fingertips across the rich lettering. He looked around the table at the faces — old and young, men and women, the variegated hues of a well-tended garden.

'This Faith,' he said at last, 'it is like a large family, isn't it?'

'May you always find it so,' said Dhikru'lláh. 'It was to nurture this family of humanity that Bahá'u'lláh came. It was for this that so many have given their all.'

10

A Fortress for Well-Being

THE next day Moayyed, Ali and Hasan went back to 'Adasíyyih, but they stayed in the village itself, not at Hormoz's house on the river. The house they used was one of the larger cottages that the owners had vacated temporarily to accommodate the expected arrival of Ali's parents.

Hasan was amazed at the efficiency of the communication among the various Bahá'í families. Somehow everyone seemed to know what everyone else was doing without being nosy and without gossiping. It was a subtle but significant distinction for Hasan. In Yazd he had often overheard devout Muslim students praising one mulla while degrading another, as if matters of religion were the province of an exclusive club, a coterie of élite scholars.

But among the Bahá'ís there was no clergy or priesthood. Only 'Abdu'l-Bahá had a position of authority, and that by virtue of His station as Exemplar and Centre of the Covenant, titles bestowed on Him by Bahá'u'lláh Himself. And yet, though 'Abdu'l-Bahá was ever regarded with the utmost reverence and respect by the Bahá'ís, He never held Himself aloof from anyone. Hasan found the paradox delightful: each Bahá'í would unhesitatingly lay down his life for 'Abdu'l-Bahá, and yet that same selfless and unassuming figure who paced the streets of Haifa rode a simple white donkey and was known and loved by everyone in Haifa and 'Akká from the simplest peasant to the highest government official.

Hasan looked forward to the visit of Uncle Husayn and Aunt Nahid. He had lived with them only a short while, but he felt loved in their household, partly because they were his closest kin. But there was something else he was beginning to recognize in his anticipation of their arrival, something he had begun to understand while staying with Hormoz and seeing the young Parsee couple live and work together in quiet harmony.

Growing up in his grandmother's house, Hasan had not been exposed to the intimate, day-to-day mechanisms of a marriage, of a complete family. His grandmother's husband had died shortly after her own children were born, and she never spoke much about him or about married life in general. Now at thirteen Hasan was beginning to marvel at the attraction and bond between husband and wife, between male and female. It excited him, something he had several times shared with Ali when they spoke of Ali's fondness for his friend Neda. At the same time, Hasan was awed by the subject, by his unexplored new feelings and by the mystery of marriage itself.

He understood human sexuality, in theory, at least. He had also read many of the classic love stories in the poetry and prose of the renowned authors of Persian literature. But even they seemed to portray the mystical force of love, the transforming affection between Layli and Majnun, as something beyond rationality or comprehension.

Observing his aunt and uncle, or Habib and Ferodeh, Hasan had sensed a relationship quite distinct from those described in the poems and stories he had read. There was humour and affection in these marriages, but he witnessed no great passion. He sensed strength and fidelity, but hardly the uncontrollable ecstasy that inevitably marked the final pages of the great stories of romance.

Where then was love? What was love that it was so rarely to be observed? Was true love only the divine attraction between God and His creation, or perhaps love was something veiled in secrecy, the exclusive privilege of lovers themselves, a private ritual? Perhaps it was merely the fiction of poets, this irresistible force that melted hearts and chastened lovers through sleepless nights?

These thoughts which had pestered Hasan over a period of time now seemed to coalesce once he heard that Ali's parents were to arrive – now that he aspired to be a Bahá'í, he might presume to ask Aunt Nahid her opinion about the subject. It would not be easy, but having been raised by his grandmother, Hasan still felt more comfortable with the idea of discussing such personal matters with a woman than with Ali or Moayyed.

The next few days went swiftly. Hasan and Ali attended classes in the morning and worked with the other families in the fields in the afternoon. Winter would soon be coming to an end, and there was much to be done to prepare the fields for spring planting.

It was difficult work, different from anything Hasan had ever done before, but it left him feeling invigorated and useful. He and Ali would clear the fields of weeds and bramble until their hands were sore. Because Hasan was not used to such work, his hands soon became blistered. At the end of the day his legs ached and his back throbbed. When he and Ali returned to the cottage each day, Hasan could smell the earth on his skin and feel the sunburn on his neck.

He looked forward to the walk home, and when they arrived, he and Ali would heat water in a large kettle on the stove and bathe in a small room behind the house. Nothing had ever felt so good, so refreshing as that warm water in the cold air of winter. Never had he slept so well as he did those nights after work, his mind free of any complex matter, his spirit satisfied with a job done well. In the morning he was awake before dawn to assemble with the others to say prayers and eat a hearty meal of cheeses, olives, fresh bread and hot tea.

It was a simple life, so remote from the cares of the world. The farmers in 'Adasíyyih were hardly impervious to the war, nor did the conflict go unmentioned. Indeed, the purpose of Husayn's visit was to help Moayyed convey the Master's instructions about storing grain to feed the victims of war in 'Akká and Haifa, those whose husbands and fathers had been conscripted into the service of the Ottoman army. But for Hasan this was a paradise, this fertile land and this community of friends.

When Uncle Husayn and Aunt Nahid came, he greeted them so joyfully and eagerly that they were amazed. Was this the same youth who had stayed with them weeks before in Abú-Sinán? Such change in so short a time seemed unthinkable, and yet there he was, his shoulders no longer stooped, his eyes no longer downcast. He was smiling, bright-eyed, tanned, and he greeted them as though they were his own parents.

They had arrived late in the afternoon, and Nahid went immediately into the kitchen to help the young woman from the village prepare the evening meal while Husayn went with Moayyed and Ali to the Ḥazíratu'l-Quds for a meeting with the village farmers. After he had washed and put on fresh clothes, Hasan sat and read for awhile until the village woman left. Then he went into the kitchen and sat on a wooden chair. He tried to think of a subtle way to introduce the subject that was on his mind, but before he could begin Nahid asked him how he had been enjoying life in the country.

The more glowing his reports, the more enthusiastic were her questions. And when he told her of his intention to become a Bahá'í, she wiped her hands on her apron and gave her young nephew a very large hug.

He blushed and was surprised to discover how much emotion she seemed to convey with that simple gesture. Her soft cheek and perfume recalled his mother's embrace so many years before. The remembrance went quickly, as a single breeze might ripple across a field of tall grasses.

She went back to her work as they talked. He helped by picking through the lentils, taking out any that were shrivelled or discoloured. Finally, when he could think of no indirect way to introduce the question, he simply blurted out, 'You and Uncle Husayn are in love, aren't you?'

Nahid laughed at first, then realized Hasan was quite serious. She immediately tried to suppress her reaction to the unexpected query.

'Why, why, yes. That is . . .' She looked at Hasan's face, trying to read what was on the boy's mind. 'We love each other very much.'

'But you're not *in* love?'

'In love? Words about love are so inadequate, Hasan. They mean one thing to one person and something else to another. When I think of being *in* love, I think of young people who have just met, who lie awake at night longing for each other.'

'Yes, that's the kind of love I am talking about!' said Hasan. 'You don't feel that?'

'You mean the romance of story-books, of poems and songs?'

'Of Majnun and Layli,' added Hasan.

Now Nahid thought she understood what her nephew was asking. 'Hasan, there is a vast difference between being in love and loving, between the ecstasy of infatuation, that first attraction of two kindred souls, and the love that grows from being nourished over years together.'

'You mean there is no such thing as the love I am talking about?'

'Oh, yes!' said Nahid. 'Certainly there is. And, of course, that is what most people think of when they talk about love or dream about love, because those initial feelings are so memorable, so over-powering, so touching to recall and so beautiful to see.' She wiped her hands, put aside her work, and sat down at the table. 'There is a phrase, "All the world loves a lover", and it's true. There is a kind of charming madness to it. But that is only the beginning of love and loving, like the first stirrings of life in the spring. Unfortunately, many people think that nothing else is love but these feelings.'

'Why is that unfortunate?' asked Hasan. To him such feelings seemed quite wonderful.

Nahid struggled in her mind for a way to explain what she meant. 'You see these little white blossoms,' she said, reaching for the vase in the centre of the table where had been placed some small branches from a newly-blooming orange tree to perfume the air. 'Look how delicate these flowering branches are. Smell the fragrant scent they share.' Hasan smelled the tiny white flowers, the sweet perfume almost like jasmine. 'If we became so fond of the flowers that we cut them every time they appeared, we might enjoy the perfume, but we would destroy the real purpose of the flower and the whole tree.'

'I don't understand,' said Hasan.

'From these flowers the fruit is begun. Through these branches the fruit is fed. The roots of the tree are planted in fertile soil and extract from the earth all the nourishment the tree needs. The leaves convert sunlight into energy, and all the efforts of the tree are bent on producing and caring for the fruit of the tree.'

'You make the tree sound like a factory,' said Hasan with a laugh.

'In a way it is, I suppose, a factory whose product is oranges. But that is why when we speak of the "fruit" of something, we mean its intended results, its very purpose.'

She showed him where some of the oranges had already begun as minuscule berries the size of a pea. 'We have cut the branch to enjoy its perfume in the house. But what would happen if we always cut the flowering branches?'

'We would never have any oranges!' said Hasan.

'That is what many people do to love,' said Nahid. 'They are so enamoured of the flowering of love that they sever the bloom to savour its beauty and never discover the fruit of love — they miss its entire purpose.'

'But the flowers die anyway,' said Hasan. 'Even if they are on the branch, they still die.'

'Yes, but they can fulfil their destiny,' said Nahid. 'Their fragrant perfume attracts the bees who pollinate the plants. The pollinated flowers produce the fruit.

'It is the same with love, Hasan. The first stages of love are bright and gay and joyous like these blossoms — that's why poets sing the praise of this flowering. No one cares about the plant when it is going about its daily task of simple growth, and yet without the daily nurturing of the plant, there would be no flowers.'

'And without the flowers there would be no fruit!' said Hasan.

'Yes, exactly. The flowering of love is fine and wonderful, but it is not the end — it is not enough.'

'Then what is?' asked Hasan. 'What is the fruit of love?'

'After all is said and done, all human progress is the fruit of love, because all love reflects and leads us to the love of God, and the heart and soul of our purpose in this life is − '

'To know and to worship God,' said Hasan, completing her thought.

'Yes, precisely, just as Bahá'u'lláh has stated it in the midday prayer. So the fruit of love is all creation. You are the fruit of your parents' love, as are all the children of the world. Humankind is the fruit of God's love. But then humanity has its own purpose, to carry forward what Bahá'u'lláh calls an "ever-advancing civilization", the fruit of constant progress and change.'

'You mean the fruit is never finished? Mankind will never reach its goal?'

'But that is the goal − to be in motion, to be moving toward perfection.' Nahid paused and struggled for the right words. 'It is the same with love. It is the same with all human attributes. If I were to ask you when a love is fulfilled, what would you say?'

Hasan thought seriously about the question for a moment, but could not think of an answer. 'I don't know. I can't imagine.'

'Because such a condition does not exist. You see, no matter how powerfully two people love or how beautifully they express that love, whether as husband and wife or as neighbours or friends, that love can always improve, always be expressed more exquisitely. Thus the fruit of the initial attraction, that first flowering of love is a growth that never stops, even though the later stages may not be as eye-catching as the flowering was.'

Hasan looked at his aunt's kind face and was enthralled by her description. 'Oh, I hope that I might find such a love one day.'

'You will if you are wise and know what you are looking for. You see, Hasan, most people speak of "falling in love" as if it were a divine accident, like stumbling on a lost treasure or −'

'Or falling out of a window,' Hasan interrupted humorously.

'Yes, perhaps that too,' said Nahid. 'But if we think of love in such a way, as a force beyond reason or will, we can excuse all sorts of immorality and irresponsibility. If we cannot control how or when we fall in love, or whom we love, and if we are powerless to resist love, then we cannot be held responsible for leaving a husband or a wife to follow someone else. What is more,' she said emphatically, 'if one can fall *in* love, one can just as easily fall *out* of love! and how would that be — this most important part of human life totally beyond our control? Does that make any sense, that God would create us so pitiful and weak?'

'You mean love is planned?'

'Not exactly. I did not say that the flowering of love does not occur, did I? It does, and it is powerful and lovely and beautiful, this unexplainable attraction between two human beings. Like a magnetic force it can draw two people together, sometimes without apparent reason or logic. We cannot always control when such attraction occurs, nor should we want to. But always remember these two things.' She took his hand as if she were impressing her thoughts into his physical being. 'First, you can grow to love someone without such an intense beginning — the flowering is not always so easily perceived. Second, we are not always attracted to the best people; therefore, how we respond to this attraction *is* fully in our power!'

'We don't have to fertilize it and nurture it?' suggested Hasan.

'Exactly!' said Nahid, truly impressed with the wisdom of one so young.

Hasan looked out the window, then at the delicate flowers on the green bough. 'I'm curious, Aunt Nahid. How could one become attracted to the wrong person?'

'Who knows? Training, background, a thousand reasons. If you lived an unhealthy life and did not eat well, you might wish to eat candy all day. Your attraction to sweets might seem overpowering. Would that mean it was good for you?'

'No,' said Hasan with a laugh, 'I guess not.'

'Of course not. I suspect that the healthier we are, the healthier will be those people who attract us. If we are trained to appreciate the spiritual aspects of others, then we will not be impressed with the purely physical exterior — we will seek out those with inner qualities.'

'But how do we find such people?' asked Hasan.

'Simple enough,' said Nahid, getting up from the table to resume her work. 'You search. Like any other worthwhile human endeavour, you must search and struggle.'

Hasan reached for the branch, then stood and walked to the window. He looked out over the rich dark fields, barely visible in the fading twilight. How he longed to be in love, to be enthralled. To have someone always there to be with, to talk to, to cherish and be cherished in return. How much time would he have to endure before he might find such a treasure?

He looked at his aunt, who was preparing rice in a large iron pot. 'The poems and stories about love,' he said, 'they don't exactly tell the truth, do they?'

'A part of the truth, perhaps. And yet many of them contain a most unfortunate lie.'

'What is that?'

'How do these stories usually end?'

'The lover fights in battles, crosses rivers, climbs mountains and finally reaches his beloved,' said Hasan.

'And then?'

'What?'

'What happens then?'

'Why, nothing. I mean, they are finally together.'

'And so?'

'The story ends.'

'It ends? Does it not seem that their union should be the beginning of a love story, not its ending?'

Hasan smiled. 'It does, doesn't it? I never thought of that. The stories say they live happily ever after.'

'But they don't ever show that happiness, do they?'

'No, they don't. Why is that?'

'Because the progress of love after the fragrant beginnings is not always exciting or adventurous. Like any important human growth, it is a process of daily attention. So the poets don't describe the husband labouring in fields or the wife comforting her sick children. They never catalogue the thousand and one adversities that are the daily fare of love.'

'No, they never do,' Hasan admitted.

'You are simply told to imagine that the same love you see as the story ends somehow endures unchanged and endless. Neither lover ever dies. Neither gets old. But think, Hasan. Could such a thing be possible?' Once again she paused in her work and turned to Hasan. ''Abdu'l-Baha has said that one major principle of all life is that everything must change. Everything is either growing or declining. That love we witness at the story's ending may indeed endure and grow and become something beyond comprehension, but it will not do so simply because the lovers are at last together. No, if it is to grow and develop, they will have to labour mightily. But one thing is absolutely certain: love cannot possibly stay the same, can it?'

'I suppose not,' Hasan confessed. 'But if that is true, why do poets write such lies?'

'Oh, perhaps their stories are not lies, Hasan. Perhaps they only tell part of the story, the part that most people want to hear. Their stories may still inspire us by demonstrating the power of affection to overcome vast obstacles. There's nothing wrong with that. And when the lovers are at long last united, it is as if they are finally secure against all forces that might pursue them, as if their union was a fortress. And it can be. Bahá'u'lláh says in one marriage prayer that the law of marriage is a ''fortress for well-being and salvation''.'

Hasan liked the image of love as a fortress – it seemed in keeping with his image of how two people should be together, and he suddenly felt very good about the whole thing. Perhaps the poets did not think the rest of the story worthwhile, but to Hasan it seemed just as special as he had imagined it might be.

'A fortress, eh?'

'Yes,' said Nahid with a smile. 'But you know,' she added, 'I have always thought that perhaps the fortress is not so much to protect us from the world at large as it is to protect us from ourselves.'

Hasan was startled by the idea. 'From ourselves?'

'Yes. You see, in some ways it would probably be easier and simpler to live life by yourself – secluded, away from the world. But such a life is a very selfish one. Bahá'u'lláh says that we are created to help build something, not retreat from society.

'In marriage one must quickly learn to be unselfish, or the marriage will falter and fail. So when I read that prayer, I always picture a fortress which is protecting me from being selfish or self-centred, a fortress against the negative part of myself.'

She resumed preparing the evening meal. Then she looked at Hasan with a large smile. 'But you are right — we need more poems about the rest of the story.'

Hasan watched Aunt Nahid for several minutes. Suddenly he felt he understood with perfect clarity why Ali was such a noble youth.

He inhaled again the sweet perfume of the orange blossoms commingled with the spicy aroma of Aunt Nahid's special rice pilaf. 'I think I know what happens in the rest of the story,' he said.

11

The Two Wings of One Bird

DURING the next several days Hasan thought about what his aunt had said. When he could, he observed his aunt and uncle together and tried to discern the subtle ways they expressed love for each other.

What he saw was not like the poems and romances. There were smiles and knowing looks, respect and kindliness, help and consideration. There was no fiery passion, no stolen glances of forbidden love. But, of course, this was not a forbidden love, not something temporary or doomed.

Not that they were always the same — sometimes there was tension, especially when they were tired or when Husayn was troubled by rumours he heard concerning possible sanctions against 'Abdu'l-Bahá by the Ottoman authorities. The persistent machinations of Muḥammad-'Alí, 'Abdu'l-Bahá's half-brother who made life miserable for all the Bahá'ís, were beginning to increase the difficulties for the Master.

When the tone of their conversation suddenly became dry and cold and there seemed to be no love there, Hasan was shocked, even frightened. He would think, 'They don't really love each other at all.' But then the next morning the tension was gone, and they acted for all the world as if nothing had happened.

Hasan studied the couple as inconspicuously as he could, and he began to realize that love and marriage were not at all the simple things that stories had led him to believe. Aunt Nahid was right, he thought; there should be stories to tell what happens after the battles are won and the hero returns. Because life did not stop there, with a welcome embrace and music and the sunset. It went on, day after day, with children and sickness, earning a living, and a myriad other things no poet had bothered to celebrate or sing.

And why? Hasan thought about it intensely. Surely this was more interesting, the daily struggle to make love transcendent. Why did it have to remain such a mystery?

One afternoon several days later, as he and Ali were working in the fields, Hasan mentioned the conversation with Aunt Nahid. He asked Ali why he thought it was that the poems and stories about love never dealt with the fruit of love, the union itself. 'All they ever talk about is what happens before the lovers get together,' said Hasan.

Ali laughed as he tossed a clump of bramble onto a handcart. 'Who would read them?'

'I would,' said Hasan.

'Yes, but poets write about things that are full of adventure and excitement. Living together day after day hardly sounds eventful.'

'But it is, isn't it? I mean, two people developing a lifelong friendship – what could be more exciting or more important than that?'

'A battle with dragons, swimming the Hellespont, travelling across the world, warring with demons – '

'All right, all right,' Hasan interrupted. 'I get the point.' He knelt down to dig up the dry roots of a plant that winter had taken. He dug a few more, but his heart was not in his work today. His mind was too curious, too full of questions.

'Ali, have you ever been in love?'

'What?' said Ali with a surprised look.

'In love,' said Hasan. 'I want to know if you have ever been in love?'

'Well, I ... I think I, ... that is, I – '

'You love Neda, don't you?' Hasan said.

'Perhaps. That is, I suppose – '

'Just say it – you love her!'

'Yes, yes. But don't tell anyone, all right?'

Hasan was silent for a moment, then he said what was really on his mind. 'Do you ever think about how strange it is the way that men and women are together in a marriage?'

'You mean physically?'

'Yes.'

'I suppose,' said Ali, surprised and a little embarrassed by his cousin's frank observation.

'I do too,' said Hasan in a barely audible tone, and he began to dig again. Ali glanced at his young cousin, but said nothing. 'I was talking with your mother a couple of days ago, about love, about marriage and everything,' said Hasan. He was too embarrassed to look up and half-heartedly continued to dig as he talked. 'It started me thinking about it, the physical part of love, I mean. I think it's strange. It's just a physical thing, but it seems to be so important to everyone.'

'Well, it's more than just a physical thing.'

'But why should the physical relationship be so important? Doesn't Bahá'u'lláh say the most important thing we do is to know and worship God? Then why does it matter how people are together physically? Does that make sense to you?'

'It does, but I'm not sure why. At least, I'm not sure I know how to explain it. For one thing, the physical relationship between a man and woman is capable of creating life. But there's something else. Father told me once that the physical part of love is a symbol of the spiritual and intellectual union of two people.'

'What do you mean?'

'Father explained it to me this way. He said that the physical union of a husband and wife is usually a reflection of the truth of their relationship, a special sort of communication reserved for the most special human relationship we can have in this life.'

'Can't there be many special relationships?'

'Well, yes, but special in other ways. Just because you are married doesn't mean you don't care about other people, but marriage is still different. I can't explain it well. You really need to talk with my father — that's who I talk to about such things.'

Hasan looked down and resumed working. 'I couldn't,' he mumbled.

'Why not?'

'Just couldn't, that's all.'

'Sure you could. He'll be here in a little while. He'd be glad to talk with you.'

Hasan did not respond and Ali did not push the matter. The truth was that Hasan was intimidated by Husayn. In fact, Hasan had rarely been able to talk comfortably with any man — the conversations with Moayyed and Dhikru'lláh were unusual for him. In Yazd, men had always been figures of authority — mullas, teachers, officers of the Shah. They were hardly the sort of people with whom one might comfortably discuss intimate concerns.

In about a half hour they saw Husayn walking up the path beside the field. Ali waved to be sure his father saw them. Husayn returned the gesture.

'Labourers in the vineyard, eh?' he called out with a laugh as he approached.

'Things must have gone well,' said Ali.

'Yes, I suppose so. Of course, there's always more to do than there is time to do it in these troubled times.'

Hasan was taken aback by his uncle's easy manner. Husayn had been quite preoccupied since Hasan's arrival, but now here he was at ease, speaking of his business affairs with his own son and in the presence of his nephew.

'Hasan and I were just talking about you,' said Ali, much to Hasan's displeasure. How dare Ali speak of their private conversation without asking first?

'We were talking about marriage,' Ali continued. 'He was asking questions I couldn't answer very well, I'm afraid.'

'Is that so?' said Husayn. He looked at Hasan who was obviously embarrassed about the whole thing. 'Well, I'm not sure I'm much of an expert myself,' said Husayn. 'Most of what I know about marriage comes from being married for almost twenty years and from what Bahá'u'lláh and 'Abdu'l-Bahá say.' He could tell Hasan was not going to volunteer any more questions.

'Tell you what, boys. You've worked hard enough for one day. Let's get some fruit and cheese and go for a hike to the river. After all the paperwork and talking I have been doing for the last two weeks, my drooping spirit needs a walk in the fresh air.'

Ali agreed enthusiastically, and Hasan, though still disturbed by what he considered Ali's breach of confidence, could hardly resist such a treat. They went by the cottage where Nahid helped them prepare a basket of delectable dates, cheese and bread. Nahid said she was unable to go because she had to help several women in the village whose children were ill. Nahid was well-respected as a healer; she had no formal training, 'just a knack', she would say, 'just the common sense my mother taught me.'

When the three reached the river it was mid-afternoon and the sun during the brief days of winter was already touching the tops of the mountains across the Jordan. They found a place on the Yarmuk not far from where it joined the Jordan River to send life-giving waters to the rest of the Holy Land.

Ali and Hasan unfolded a groundcloth while Husayn unpacked the basket for their afternoon snack. By now Hasan's anger had subsided. As they walked, Hasan listened to the ease with which his cousin talked to his father. It was always respectful, but it was clear Ali felt perfectly comfortable sharing his thoughts and feelings with Husayn. For him to tell his father about the conversation with Hasan was not in Ali's mind a breach of confidence, simply a natural course of events – to share the dilemma of a friend with another friend.

Hasan began to realize that his impression of his uncle had been completely wrong, tainted to a degree by Hasan's own observations of the relationship between the fathers and sons he had known in Yazd. So often fathers in Yazd seemed aloof and authoritarian.

But the generalizations he had formed about family interaction from his experience in Persia among non-Bahá'í families did not seem to apply to the Bahá'ís. It was true that most of them brought with them the habits and traditions of their homeland, itself shaped by centuries of Islamic culture and attitudes. But it was also clear to even the casual observer that these Bahá'í families were being quickly transformed by the teachings of their religion, teachings which emphasized consultation instead of authoritarianism, love instead of fear, knowledge instead of imitation.

Husayn spoke of these things on the walk, how he and his father had rarely conversed openly, how the explanations of 'Abdu'l-Bahá had profoundly affected the way he and Nahid had raised Ali.

'My father and I never talked,' he admitted quite candidly. 'He commanded and I obeyed. Of course, I knew he loved me, though I don't recall that he ever said so.'

Hasan was utterly shocked by the frank disclosures of his uncle. Could this be the same man whom he had perceived to be severe and officious? Hasan could almost begrudge Ali his upbringing, to have the luxury of such constant companionship.

When they were seated and were enjoying the food that Nahid had prepared, Hasan found himself completely at ease once again, and once again he was amazed that his emotions could change so quickly and so completely. It unnerved him a little, these powerful shifts in mood that swept over him like summer storms. But if he could not rely on his emotions, he was beginning to trust his intellect and he was also beginning to have increasing confidence in his new family and their concern for his welfare.

It was several minutes into the conversation as they sat there on the river bank that Hasan realized how his uncle's comments about fathers and sons, about families in general were responding to the very questions Hasan had asked Nahid and Ali. But instead of perceiving this coincidence as some conspiracy of hearts, he received the attention as it was intended — an expression of familial affection. After all, he was now part of their family, and like any family member, his problems were their problems and could be pursued with frank and open consultation.

'As a matter of fact,' Husayn was saying, 'I have thought a great deal about what a family is supposed to be.' His voice was mingled with the rippling water that meandered through the flood plain ferrying twigs and dead leaves downstream from the awakening fields. 'I suppose I have come to believe that a family is much more than a practical way to organize human society. I have come to think of a family as a school, a place for training humanity for God's purposes, a school of love.'

He leaned back so that his arms supported his back and lifted his face as if he were basking in the fresh air. 'You know,' he continued, 'the Master has said that "Love is the greatest law in this vast universe of God." He says it is "the universal magnetic power" that attracts one thing to another, the force that makes the planets stay in their orbits, that organizes human society.'

He adjusted himself again so that he could see both boys, and he placed his hands together to emphasize the unity he was describing. 'You see, it is in the family that we first learn to love one another and are introduced to our primary purpose in this life − to know and to love God. Because that's what love is all about − when we love someone, we are actually attracted magnetically to the godly virtues they possess.'

'Is all love like that?' asked Hasan.

'What do you mean, son?'

'The love in story-books, and even . . . well, physical love. Is that also a love of God?'

Husayn smiled. 'Not everything that people call love is truly love − that is certain. When 'Abdu'l-Bahá was in London He spoke about love. He said that "the love which sometimes exists between friends is not love, because it is subject to transmutation", that is, to change. He said, " . . . this is merely fascination. As the breeze blows the slender trees yield. If the wind is in the East the tree leans to the West, and if the wind turns to the West the tree leans to the East. This kind of love is originated by the accidental conditions of life. This is not love, it is merely acquaintanceship; it is subject to change."

'Now understand,' Husayn continued, 'He did not mean that

romantic love or passion are not real or valid emotions. But I believe
He was saying the sort of intense feelings that come and go without
reason or control are hardly worthy of the same respect that we give
to a relationship developed through tests and struggle. But you see, all
love, even the love we have for animals and nature, partakes of the
whole principle of love itself.'

'What is that?' asked Ali. 'What do you mean "the principle of
love"?'

'Bahá'u'lláh says that all creation reflects the qualities of the
Creator, what we sometimes call the virtues or attributes of God.'

'Even rocks?' asked Hasan.

'Potentially, yes, even rocks,' said Husayn. 'Because all loves, all
affection, all attractions to things or people, are potentially valuable,
are "real" love if they teach us about the higher forms of love.'

'What are they?' asked Hasan. 'What are the "higher forms" of
love?'

'Well, an ancient Greek philosopher once described it as a "ladder
of love".'

'Why is that?' asked Ali.

'It's simple,' his father continued. 'As a young child you understand love only in terms of your parents. Then as you develop you
might understand love in terms of affection for a pet. Later you learn
to care for playmates – your world of loved ones is always expanding. Because as you learn how to treat loved ones, as you progress in
your understanding of gentleness, respect, kindness, you ascend the
ladder of love, you learn to love more and more creatures in ever more
complex ways.'

'Like the farmers of 'Adasíyyih,' said Hasan, suddenly grasping
his uncle's intent, 'they are expressing their love of humanity by
growing crops to feed people.'

'That's precisely what I mean,' said Husayn, placing his hand on
his nephew's shoulder. 'The higher the form of love, the more selfless
it is, but all love has the capacity to lead us to a love of God. The
Master says that, "Real love is the love which exists between God and
His servants, the love which binds together holy souls. This is the love

of the spiritual world, not the love of physical bodies and organisms.'' Of course, in this life we express our love in physical ways, though it is not the physical being that we love.'

'That's what I am not clear about,' said Hasan. 'How can you say you love someone and yet say it is not the body that you love? Aren't they the same thing?'

'Not really,' said Husayn. 'Take your aunt and me, for example. Do you think she would love me less if a finger was severed from my hand?'

'Certainly not,' laughed Hasan.

'What about an entire hand?'

'No.'

'Or a foot?'

'Not any part,' said Hasan.

'Because it isn't my body she cherishes, but the whole person. In fact, the affection we have for each other has very little to do with our physical selves — our bodies are merely the instruments through which our souls find expression.'

'Like mirrors,' said Hasan, recalling Moayyed's analogy.

'Yes, like mirrors of the soul,' Husayn responded with a smile. 'So you see, they are important, these bodies of ours. Without them we would not be able to communicate our thoughts and feelings, at least not in this life. But without the soul, the personality, the spiritual aspect of ourselves, there would be very little in us worthwhile to care about.'

Husayn examined the faces of these eager young lads and struggled within to find the words to explain in simple terms what was hardly simple at all. 'This lesson sounds so simple; the words come so easily,' he continued, 'but for young lovers enthralled by their longing, words of reason have little value — the songs, the poems, the birds of the heart, only these speak to lovers' ears. The first stages of love are sometimes so intense, so blinding, that lovers cannot distinguish between the body and the soul. They are hardly aware that the attraction they feel is to the spirit of the beloved and not to the physical being that is the fit vehicle for that soul.'

Husayn paused again and looked into Hasan's eyes to detect if understanding were there. 'What all of us ultimately discover,' he continued, 'whether we love a husband or wife, whether we love our children, our fellow Bahá'ís, humanity as a whole, or the magnificent beauty of nature, is that we are being drawn to the names of God that are so clearly resplendent in the physical forms of this life. Indeed, Bahá'u'lláh Himself has said, "Know thou that every created thing is a sign of the revelation of God," and likewise He has said, "No thing have I perceived, except that I perceived God within it, God before it, or God after it."'

'I don't understand what that means,' said Hasan.

'Nor I,' echoed Ali.

'It means that at the heart of all things beautiful is a lesson to be learned about the divine attributes. So it is with the physical love shared between a man and woman. What is this union but the dramatic expression of spiritual affinity. By themselves, physical actions mean less than nothing unless they are used as they were intended – to convey spiritual messages. But if the young lovers do not become aware of this reality, if they are not trained to recognize what it is that attracts them, or if they are not trained so as to be attracted to attributes of God, then they may not be attracted to something or someone that is spiritually healthy for them, and the affinity is doomed.'

'But if one is attracted to the qualities of God in others,' asked Ali, 'then how could we be attracted to something unhealthy.'

Husayn shifted and became more erect. 'People are attracted to whatever they are trained to adore. If you were not educated so as to admire qualities of the spirit, you might find it very difficult to recognize those qualities in others, just as someone who has never read a book would find it difficult to discover good literature. And since none of us is perfect, we must examine what attracts us to be sure we are being drawn to the enduring spiritual qualities within another.'

'Then there is nothing wrong with physical love?' asked Hasan, now sufficiently comfortable with his uncle to ask the question that was at the heart of his other queries.

'Not so long as it is tended carefully as a gardener would nurture the most delicate plants in his garden.'

'I don't understand again,' said Ali with a laugh.

'The able gardener knows well the laws for raising his young plants, for these are the laws of nature that he must follow — when to water, how much to water, how much light to give the tender plant, what kind of soil it requires. These are not things the gardener decides — these are unchanging laws of nature he must become aware of.

'So it is with love between a man and woman. If the delicate plant of love is to grow and reach fruition, the young lovers must be aware of what laws govern the nurturing of their love. These laws Bahá'u'lláh has given us — the laws of chastity, of engagement, of marriage, of consultation and many others. All these laws describe how love can best prosper. If these laws are ignored, the affection the lovers first feel, even if it is a healthy attraction, will wither as surely as will a bud severed from the stem.'

There was silence as the cousins looked at each other, exhilarated by the prospect of what their own futures might hold. Then Ali asked his father with deepest respect, 'What laws have you found to be most important, Father?'

Surprised by Ali's frankness, Husayn thought for a moment. It was a difficult question. 'They are all important, son, whether they are specific laws or simply the guiding principles for daily life that we find in the teachings of Bahá'u'lláh. But I will tell you a couple that have meant a great deal to me. First, remember that no matter how close two people become, how much in love they are, how interdependent their lives, they remain separate and independent souls. Each one is still responsible for his or her own spiritual growth. In one of the marriage prayers revealed by 'Abdu'l-Bahá is a quotation from the Qur'án which says that in marriage God "hath let loose the two seas, that they meet each other: Between them is a barrier which they overpass not."

'Another principle I always try to keep in mind is what Bahá'u'lláh and 'Abdu'l-Bahá have said about the equality of men and women as it concerns the subtle and often difficult way that two lovers must become two partners in life's venture. At the heart of love must be mutual respect, mutual affection, and mutual regard. This equality in the partnership is as vital to the nurturing of love as is air to living creatures.'

'Why is that?' asked Ali.

'Because love cannot abide selfishness,' said Husayn. 'Because this is a partnership and cannot be centred around the desires and needs of one person alone. It may be that the man and the woman will have different duties, but they are spiritually equal and equal in authority in their marriage.'

'But is that really true, Father?' asked Ali, thinking about the Bahá'í marriages he had observed. 'Aren't most of the affairs of the Bahá'í community run by men?'

'That is true for now,' said Husayn. 'But remember this, when people become Bahá'ís they are not suddenly new people. They must struggle every day with their new awareness to become something different. The same holds true for the Bahá'í community. The more we understand the principles of the Bahá'í teachings, the more completely we will be able to put them into practice. For now, much of the Bahá'í community is shaped by its past, by the cultural background of its members or by the society in which the Bahá'ís live.

'I never thought of that,' said Ali. 'I guess I have imagined that all the Bahá'ís were just like the Bahá'ís I have known here in 'Akká.'

'Think of it this way,' continued Husayn. 'Most of us Bahá'ís here in Syria have come from Muslim countries, so naturally we are affected by our heritage, by our traditions. And yet by studying the teachings of our Faith, we have already begun to change. In the future we will change much more.'

Ali had never before heard his father speak so frankly of these things, though he himself had often wondered about how, in spite of the law of equality of sexes, men seemed still to dominate the decision-making in some Bahá'í families.

'Is that why there will be no women on the House of Justice?' asked Ali.

'No,' said Husayn. 'That is a different matter altogether. That is a permanent condition, but it has absolutely nothing to do with equality of the sexes.'

'Then what is the reason?' asked Hasan.

'We do not yet know,' Husayn answered. 'It is something we do not yet have the knowledge to comprehend. We only know that whatever the reason, it will eventually be made unquestionably clear.'

'But I thought we were not supposed to accept our beliefs blindly,' said Ali. 'I thought we were supposed to discover the reason behind the teachings of God.'

Husayn placed his hand on Ali's shoulder. 'And so we are, but once you have investigated thoroughly and have determined beyond a doubt that Bahá'u'lláh is the Manifestation for this day and that 'Abdu'l-Bahá is the Centre of His Covenant, you can believe them when they say that this matter will be made clear, especially when all the other laws and teachings confirm the principle of equality.'

'But how can it *not* have something to do with equality?' asked Hasan. 'It is a job that only men are allowed to do. Is that equal?'

'Equality is a subtle thing,' said Husayn. 'It does not mean sameness. You and Ali have different capacities, different skills and virtues. You are hardly the same, yet you are equal, are you not? It does not mean that one is better than another when we acknowledge that there are differences between two people. A man can never bear children nor can his initial relationhship with his child possibly be as intimate as that of the mother because the role of the mother is distinct and special in the first stage of a child's development. And yet we do not say that men are therefore less than women. No, men and women are equal spiritually and intellectually, but there are still differences between them.'

'What other principles of marriage should we especially know?' asked Ali, thinking in his own heart about Neda, though he would not have admitted it to anyone.

'I'll tell you one more; then it is time we started back,' said Husayn. 'It has to do with a passage in a prayer by the Master. Referring to the same analogy that Muḥammad uses about people in a marriage being like two seas, 'Abdu'l-Bahá prays, ''Make Thou this marriage to bring forth coral and pearls.''' Husayn paused. 'You have seen both, Ali, both coral and pearls. Do you have any idea what this analogy may mean?'

Ali thought long and hard, as did Hasan. 'A pearl comes from inside a rough shell,' said Hasan. 'Does it have anything to do with that?'

'A pearl comes from a grain of sand,' offered Ali.

'Very good, both of you, except you haven't explained the rest. Go ahead, Ali, tell me how the grain of sand becomes a pearl.'

'A bit of sand gets into the oyster. It irritates the membrane inside so that the oyster covers the rough sand with smooth layers of tissue, and these build up over a period of time, and . . .'

'And the result is a thing of rare beauty, you see?'

'Not really,' admitted Ali.

'If we liken the irritating grains of sand to the trials of everyday life, then we see how we can make something strong and beautiful through these tests if we will only respond to the things that provoke us with kindness and love.'

'And the coral,' asked Hasan, delighted by his uncle's explanation of the prayer, 'what does that mean?'

'Tell me how the coral is formed, my young scientist,' he said to Ali.

'I'm not exactly sure,' Ali answered. 'I know that at first the coral is alive — each little cell of it is a living creature. Then they die and get hard.'

'Yes, each layer builds on the skeleton of the past so that the coral gets larger and larger and ever more beautiful and elaborate in time.'

'But what does that have to do with marriage?' asked Hasan.

'Bahá'u'lláh says that humankind has been brought forth on this planet to produce an ever-advancing civilization, does He not? Well, this progress does not occur in the palaces or parliaments of the world. It happens day by day as the hard-won wisdom of one generation is passed on to the next and each life builds on the knowledge and sacrifice of those who went before. This gradual fashioning of a beautiful and spiritualized civilization occurs nowhere else but in families as, life by life, the children build on what their parents have learned. Without such families no progress could occur.'

As they walked back Hasan and Ali said little. They considered what Husayn had said and what it might mean in their own lives. But as they neared the house Hasan observed, 'I guess it is not easy to understand love, is it?'

'No, it isn't,' said Husayn.

12

The Mystery of Faith

A WEEK later Nahid and Husayn returned to Abú-Sinán, leaving the boys with Moayyed to help with the work and enjoy the countryside in 'Adasíyyih. Time passed quickly for Hasan as winter gave way to spring. He seemed to change almost daily. He worked in the fields and went to school with the Bahá'í boys his age — he still did not consider himself officially a Bahá'í, but more and more he felt a part of this community.

He participated eagerly in discussions about religion. More than anything else, he enjoyed the frequent conversations with Moayyed and listening to the others describe how they came to be Bahá'ís. Many had been raised by Bahá'í parents, but a number, especially among the older Bahá'ís, had joined the religion in Iran at great peril to their lives. Some had been disowned by their Muslim families or had barely escaped death at the hands of fanatical mobs.

From these Bahá'ís, and from his cousin Ali, Hasan learned about the early days of the Faith in Iran, about the Báb, the Letters of the Living, about the battles of Fort Ṭabarsí, Zanján and Nayríz, about the heroic lives of Quddús, Mullá Ḥusayn, and Ṭáhirih. And the more he learned, the more certain he became in his own mind that becoming a Bahá'í was only a matter of time for him.

And yet, partially as a result of these discussions, there was one last thing he determined he must do before he could commit himself to this decision. He wanted to see the Master, 'Abdu'l-Bahá. He was not exactly sure why this was so important to him, but part of this desire had to do with the station of 'Abdu'l-Bahá, designated by His Prophet Father as Centre of the Covenant, as Head of the Faith. In truth, Hasan's determination was not a reasoned decision, rather something of the heart derived from his deepest instincts.

No doubt he was influenced by the transforming effect that 'Abdu'l-Bahá seemed to have on all who met Him — it seemed to Hasan they could talk of little else. It was as if their lives before that event had no real significance. Yet Hasan still harboured a wariness concerning figures of authority, regardless of how benign they might appear to others. He wanted to witness for himself how such a powerful influence might radiate from one elderly, unpretentious man, how such a one could so quickly become the centre of the universe for these diverse people.

For a long while Hasan did not dare express his desire to Moayyed or even to Ali. He feared they would think him presumptuous — how could he, a youth and a stranger in their midst, deign to question the authority of the Head of their Faith? But all of this changed one evening as Moayyed told him how the noted scholar Mírzá Abu'l-Faḍl became a Bahá'í. Two months before on 21st January, the believers had gathered to commemorate the anniversary of the passing of this revered man, and as they shared stories about him, several had alluded to the special humility the former Muslim scholar had demonstrated by becoming a Bahá'í. It was only now that Hasan presumed to ask Moayyed what they had been talking about.

Moayyed described how widely respected Mírzá Abu'l-Faḍl had been among the mullas before he became a Bahá'í. He had been aware of the Bahá'ís, but he had never seriously considered the truth of this new religion. Then one day he met a simple blacksmith, Ustád Ḥusayn-i-Na'l Band. The unlettered smith approached the esteemed scholar and asked if it were not true according to Muslim tradition that each drop of rain is accompanied by an angel from heaven. The bemused scholar replied that indeed such was the case. The smith then

asked if it were not also true according to another tradition that an
angle will never visit a house with a dog in it. Again Mírzá Abu'l-Faḍl
agreed. 'Does it not follow, then,' the smith observed, 'that rain
should never fall on a house which has a dog inside?'

Moayyed described how Mírzá 'Abu'l-Faḍl was stunned by the wit
and wisdom of this unlearned man. When he discovered that this
unschooled craftsman was a Bahá'í, he determined to investigate the
religion for himself.

'Such was the humility of this man,' Moayyed concluded, 'that his
heart could be touched by the faith of a lowly smith.'

To Hasan the story meant that even he, a youth, had the right to ask
questions and that, at least among the Bahá'ís, his queries would not
be deemed heretical or born of obstinacy, but seen as a sincere
struggle to gain understanding. And so it was on an evening in late
March that Hasan told Moayyed of his desire to meet 'Abdu'l-Bahá.
Moayyed said nothing at the time. He simply smiled and nodded his
head as if to indicate that it was an understandable request, but most
likely a hopeless one.

'Abdu'l-Bahá lived simply. He had sacrificed His life utterly in
service to Bahá'u'lláh and in the twenty-three years since to the Faith
itself. He took with complete seriousness and devotion the station His
Father had bestowed on Him as Centre of the Covenant, as
Interpreter of Bahá'u'lláh's writings, and as Exemplar of the Faith.
Years before in a talk to Western pilgrims visiting Him in 'Akká,
'Abdu'l-Bahá had exhorted them to personal reformation by saying,
'Look at Me, follow Me, be as I am; take no thought for yourselves
or your lives, whether ye eat or whether ye sleep, whether ye are
comfortable, whether ye are well or ill, whether ye are with friends or
foes, whether ye receive praise or blame.'

Most of the Bahá'ís were thoroughly obedient to the instruction of
'Abdu'l-Bahá, but He constantly exhorted them in person and in his
writings to pursue their spiritual training on their own, to prepare
themselves to persevere with their beliefs even should He no longer be
among them physically. He said this more often now because His life
was beginning to be jeopardized by the menacing Ottoman official

Jamál Páshá who a year later in 1916 would vow to crucify 'Abdu'l-Bahá.

Hasan inferred the selfless love 'Abdu'l-Bahá showered upon all, Bahá'ís and non-Bahá'ís alike. He did not doubt the qualities 'Abdu'l-Bahá possessed. He only knew that meeting 'Abdu'l-Bahá would provide him with the final proof of what in some ways remained for him a noble theory. Hasan desperately wanted it to be true, though he knew such a meeting would test whether he was sufficiently worthy to be energized by this redeeming force and whether he dared confront the demands of such a belief should they be confirmed.

Throughout April Hasan felt this desire growing within him. For all intents and purposes he lived a Bahá'í life, associated with Bahá'ís, read and studied the writings of Bahá'u'lláh, was solaced by the beauteous prayers revealed by Him. But his determination would not abate. Then in May a propitious turn of events began. Word came that the Bahá'ís could move back to Haifa and 'Akká from their retreats in Abú-Sinán and the other villages.

Of course, the Bahá'ís who lived permanently in the settlements around the lake remained, and more than one family volunteered to have Hasan stay with them. But Moayyed told the boys to gather their things in preparation for the return.

'However,' he informed Ali with a laugh, 'we must take a round-about way!'

'Through Nazareth?' asked Ali excitedly.

'Exactly!' said Moayyed.

Ali later explained to Hasan how he had longed to see Nazareth again ever since his teacher Mr Bushrú'í had taught him about the life of Christ. Now he would have his chance to see this ancient city.

Hasan was not at all sure he wanted to return to 'Akká, where he had spent only a few days. To him the countryside around 'Adasíyyih had become his new home. As the day neared, his anxiety grew and his spirits drooped.

The evening before their departure, there was a great feast. Many fond embraces were shared and tears were shed. It was not so much remorse for the boys' departure — after all, 'Akká was not so far away. Rather it seemed the end of a special time, a period of intense intimacy and love, of working together to lay the foundation for an enterprise which would never again consist of a few family and friends banded together.

To Hasan's surprise, he was given a touching gift by the assembled Bahá'ís. Dhikru'lláh made a brief but heartfelt speech about the joy of seeing this 'bright young mind on the verge of its awakening'. Then Hormoz gave Hasan a photograph in a beautifully-crafted gold frame. The picture itself showed 'Abdu'l-Bahá sitting on a leather couch, His hands resting in His lap, His aspect serious but not severe. In His right hand, hanging there conspicuously, was a string of prayer beads.

'I cherish this picture,' said Hormoz, as he handed Hasan the gift. 'It always serves to remind me — if the Master on whom we depend must say so many prayers for strength and guidance, then how many more must I need say.'

Hasan could say nothing as the finely-tooled frame was placed in his hands. His eyes welled up with tears, but he did not cry. He looked at the picture, transfixed by eyes that seemed aimed at his most secret heart, by that transforming face chiselled by time and pain as an ancient oak might wear its scars. In a simple 'abá and táj, the white-bearded figure seemed to ask a question that could melt the most hardened heart or calloused spirit.

That night Hasan slept with the picture beside him. He had seen portraits of 'Abdu'l-Bahá before in the homes of the Bahá'ís he had visited, but none quite like this, none that seemed to speak to him as this did.

The next morning they left early after dawn prayers. The wagon crossed the river and at the village of Kinneret headed up the mountains toward Nazareth which lay on the Haifa road. Often as they rode, the morning sun behind them, Hasan looked back, his hands cupped over his eyes that he might see the beautiful lake and the villages that seemed so small at a distance, so insignificant.

It was unthinkable to him that only six months had passed since he had first seen the lake. For the first time he began to realize, as he remembered his feelings the day he arrived at Tiberias, what those around him had noted so often in his presence – how much he had changed in a few short months.

He could not detect so easily as they how many ways he had grown – the strengthening of his arms and shoulders, the brightening of his face. But he could remember vividly the fears, the tenuousness that seemed at the time as inseparable a part of him as his own name. Yet here he was, strong, tanned, capable, well-liked, more sure of himself than he had ever been before.

They reached Nazareth that afternoon, stopping at a distance from the town to enjoy the view.

'It's not at all as I remembered,' said Ali.

'Oh?' said Moayyed. 'How is that?'

'I remembered a simple village, the way it is described in the Bible.'

'That was two thousand years ago,' said Moayyed. 'Besides, places and people are rarely the way we remember them – our imaginations and desires too often make them into what we wish them to be.'

'What do you mean?' asked Hasan quickly, thinking somehow Moayyed was referring to his own notions about 'Abdu'l-Bahá.

'What? Oh, simply that we have to be careful how much stock we place in our preconceptions about things.' He adjusted himself so that he was facing Hasan. 'I remember the first time I saw the city of Jerusalem. From a distance it was quite beautiful. From the hills surrounding the city I could see the Dome of the Rock covering the site where Abraham brought his son Ishmael, the same site where Muḥammad is supposed to have ascended to heaven. I thought to myself that here was the very hill where David's Temple once stood so proud and majestic. And of course I could see so many places associated with the ministry and life of Christ – the Mount of Olives where he preached, the garden of Gethsemane where he prayed.

'And yet, the closer I got,' he continued, as he motioned with his hand, 'the more the city seemed to be a morass of confusion and contention. Instead of discovering in this holy place the common bond of faith, religions there seem to vie for the right to possess these sacred places. Even within the same religion there are disputes, some saying Christ was crucified in one place, others vehemently saying it was elsewhere, and each division within the religion dividing up these edifices and the earth itself in order to possess a separate plot, a few square metres that they may claim to separate themselves from the other religions.

'Years later I heard 'Abdu'l-Bahá say that if religion becomes the source of dissension and division, it is useless and dead. Well, that day as I wandered through the streets of that anicent city I felt no unity, no love, no spiritual awakening. I could not feel comfort in knowing what holy feet had trod those ancient paths. For me Jerusalem was like a garbage heap of history, layer upon layer of useless relics, ancient walls that men had devised to avoid becoming unified with the rest of humanity.

'A man I was with at the time, himself a Jew, perceived my consternation. He said to me, "Do not blame this holy city for what the blind and ignorant may do to it. Long after they have gone and their petty squabbles are lost to the memory of man, Jerusalem will remain here as a remembrance of God, as a proof that God has not left us without guidance.'''

'I guess that's what I feel,' said Ali. 'I expected something different.'

'Outward circumstances cannot change our hearts,' said Moayyed, 'not unless we choose to let them. Enjoy these hallowed spots for what they are, remembrances of God. Try not to let your spirits be dampened by what people have done to them in their ignorance. There is a difference between acquiring information and acquiring wisdom. The religion of God is not hard to understand − it is divinely simple. But there is a ḥadíth Bahá'u'lláh quotes in *The Seven Valleys* that says, "Knowledge is a single point, but the ignorant have multiplied it." And one of the Hidden Words of Bahá'u'lláh says: "O ye that are foolish, yet have a name to be wise! Wherefore do ye wear the guise of shepherds,when inwardly ye have become wolves, intent upon My flock?"'

'I don't understand,' said Hasan.

'The truth about religion is simple − just as you noted − it is like a single point. But the ignorant who fail to see the simple unity of religion, who exalt one Prophet over another or contend that only their beliefs offer the correct understanding of divine truth, these people create division out of unity and discord from harmony. They make the single point many points. And yet these very ones are often those who have a name to be wise − the leaders of religion, the judges, the kings, the learned. Through their own selfishness or mischievousness or in their innocent blindness, they injure the very people they purport to guide and assist.'

'I'm not sure I understand how someone can be very intelligent and learned and not understand a simple truth,' said Ali.

'Because it is also a matter of the heart,' said Hasan, thinking about his own belief.

'Why, yes,' said Moayyed, once again astonished at Hasan's remarkable understanding. 'In the final analysis, it all depends on spiritual perception, and no one can ever guess who has it and who does not, or what subtle combination of qualities enables one person to see and understand while another does not.'

The old man and his two charges talked a while longer, and then went into the city to see for themselves the array of churches, each with its own special version of the religion of Christ and the meaning of Christ's teachings. They saw the Roman Catholic Church of the Annunciation, built on the site where the Archangel Gabriel was supposed to have appeared to the Virgin Mary to inform her she was to be the mother of a Prophet of God. They saw the Greek Orthodox church called the Church of Gabriel where, the members of that faith contend, the Annunciation occurred. They saw the Synagogue Church built where Christ once preached in the synagogue, as well as the church at the Workshop of Joseph where Christ's father was supposed to have had his carpentry shop.

By sunset the three were exhausted and eagerly retired to the inn where they would stay for the night. After dinner Ali went immediately to bed and was quickly asleep. But Hasan, who was no less tired, stayed awake in order to have a few moments alone with Moayyed.

When Moayyed finished his prayers and sat on the edge of his bed winding up an old alarm clock he took with him so that he could always get up for dawn prayers, Hasan quietly stepped over to the bed and sat down, the cherished portrait of 'Abdu'l-Bahá in his hands.

'Sir,' he said softly, 'I want to see 'Abdu'l-Bahá – I really believe I *must* see Him.'

'Oh?' said Moayyed, placing his arm around his beloved Hasan. 'And why is that?'

'I cannot tell you, but I must.'

Moayyed sensed immediately that this most personal of matters should not be questioned.

'Very well,' he said. 'I will see what can be done. We will arrive in Haifa tomorrow. I will make inquiries.'

Hasan was taken aback. He had not expected such a thing to occur any time soon, if at all, and suddenly this crucial and climactic event loomed as much a threat as a bounty to him.

'But ... I ...'

'Yes?'

'I am ... worried.' He wanted to say *afraid*, but it seemed a strange thing to say.

'About what?'

'What if ... what if I ...' He struggled for the words. 'What if He is ... different?'

'Different? How different? In what way?'

'What if I do not believe Him to be as wonderful and perfect as everyone else seems to think? You know how you were telling us today what you felt when you went to Jerusalem? What if I feel nothing and ... well, what if I am not meant to believe?'

'Not *meant* to believe? Hasan, my dearest one, you misunderstood me. Belief is not an accident. It does not depend on the emotions you might feel on one occasion.'

'But when I was talking some weeks ago with Aunt Nahid and Uncle Husayn about love, they were saying that we may control how we respond to our attraction to people, but we cannot always determine who attracts us.'

'There is more than one way of being attracted, Hasan. In some countries marriages are arranged by parents. That does not mean there is no love or attraction in these marriages. You fear that you may not be enthralled by 'Abdu'l-Bahá, but you already are!' Moayyed pointed to the picture that Hasan cradled in his hands.

'You mean this picture?'

'No, I mean the Faith itself. Do you not love the teachings of this religion?'

'Of course I do. I have told you so many times. I love the beliefs and I love the Bahá'ís themselves.'

'Then you love 'Abdu'l-Bahá, because these beliefs and this religion are the heart and soul of 'Abdu'l-Bahá, what He has devoted every minute of his life to.

'How do you think He became called 'Abdu'l-Bahá? Some would have placed Him on a par with Bahá'u'lláh, would have deemed Him a Prophet. Others accused Him of trying to assume the station of Bahá'u'lláh. He put to rest all such speculation by adopting a name which describes Him as a servant, a servant to His Father, a servant to this Faith, and a servant to the servants of God — 'Abdu'l-Bahá. But let me not lecture you, Hasan. Your fears will vanish soon enough. Instead, let me share this thought — not all who met the Prophets understood. Many met Bahá'u'lláh without suspecting He was a Manifestation. They saw only a man. But you already have faith because you have studied and believed.

'I remember so clearly when I was a young man on a pilgrimage to the house of the Báb in Shíráz, the place where the Báb declared Himself to Mullá Husayn. For months I had planned this journey, and, as the time neared, I was unable to eat or sleep, so intense was my excitement.

'Then the day came. After a long journey I entered the door and climbed those hallowed steps to the upper room. It was quiet and beauteous, so utterly tranquil. There were other Bahá'ís there, even though we had to be very discreet, and as I approached the threshold to that chamber I saw four or five other pilgrims kneeling, softly chanting prayers, but with such fervour, such devotion that the room seemed to vibrate with the pitch of their voices. Most of them were in tears, so enthralled were they at attaining this most cherished spot.

'Suddenly I became aware that I was merely observing them − I myself felt nothing − at least, not at all what I thought I should feel, certainly nothing like what these other souls were experiencing.'

'What did you do?'

'I could do nothing. I was seized with consternation. It passed through me like an icy dart. I felt as though every ounce of strength had suddenly drained from me. I was terrified. Had I lost my faith? Was I unworthy?

'I dropped to my knees to pray, but I could not pray − I was too upset to concentrate. The words were just words. Immediately I got up and left the room. I went down the stairs and out into the court-yard beneath the shade of the orange tree the Báb Himself had planted there. I felt shattered, as though all I had worked for in my life was suddenly hollow and meaningless.

'Then, almost imperceptibly at first, there was a whistling sound coming from the doorway. Out stepped an elderly gentleman whom I recognized as the caretaker of the house, a devoted believer of many years. He was going about his task of sweeping the passageways. I cannot tell you how it shocked me to hear him, to see him.'

'But why?'

'Because, Hasan, here he was, constantly in the presence of this holy spot, and yet he was hardly in the throes of passionate emotion. He was not crying. He was not on his knees praying. Yet he was joyful, so obviously joyful.

'Just then, the other pilgrims began to emerge into the courtyard. There were men and women, young and old. Some were from Shíráz, but most were from faraway cities. Instantly my heart melted with joy and consolation.'

'I don't understand,' said Hasan.

'Because, my son, *this* was the proof of my belief, not fleeting emotions from a visit to a single room, but the living, breathing, revitalized souls touched by the power of this Cause, come from great distances, some at peril to their very lives, just to visit this simple house. These were the signs of my faith!'

'Did you go back in and feel as they did?' asked Hasan, longing for a neat, happy ending to the story.

'No,' said Moayyed. 'Not that day I didn't. I did not need to. That's the point. In the final analysis, faith is not a mystery, not really, so do not fear that something beyond your power can ever take it away.'

'Can I at least be nervous about it?' asked Hasan.

'That I will allow,' said Moayyed. 'But for now you must rest — tomorrow might be the most important day in your life.'

'What do you mean?'

'Well, every day has that possibility, doesn't it?'

13

The Face of the Master

FOR several weeks 'Abdu'l-Bahá had been holding weekly gatherings in Haifa. He would meet with the believers and recount for them stories about the lives of the faithful souls who had given their all to the Cause of God. These verbal sketches were not long. In succinct anecdotes 'Abdu'l-Bahá would highlight the special traits that had distinguished the services of these individuals. He told of the well-known heroes and heroines, like Ṭáhirih and Nabíl-i-Zarandí, but he also told stories of less well-known figures like Ustád 'Alí-Akbar-i-Najjár, the cabinet maker, and 'Abdu'ṣ-Ṣálih, the gardener of the Riḍván.

These biographical sketches inevitably inspired the assembled listeners much more than any abstract dictums might have done because they provided concrete examples – real lives devoted to God, tested through tribulation, and exalted through a belief fleshed out with deeds. When Moayyed had received word that one of these meetings was to be held the evening of their arrival, he decided there could be no better time for Hasan to fulfil his heart's desire.

At first Moayyed thought to make up excuses why he and Ali could not accompany Hasan to the home of 'Abdu'l-Bahá, but he decided the boy was bright enough to understand.

'This is your time,' he told him, recalling his own experience at the house of the Báb. 'You must take from this meeting what is yours and not concern yourself about what anyone else there may be thinking about you.'

Hasan was not sure he understood or agreed, but he accepted the gesture as it was intended, a token of Moayyed's affection and respect. In any case, he was much too preoccupied to be worried about such matters.

As the carriage approached the city of Haifa, a small settlement just starting to grow into what 'Abdu'l-Bahá said would some day become a sprawling metropolis, Hasan became anxious. It was one thing to confront the veracity of words on paper, to test theories and ideas, even to witness those theories in the actions of followers, but to come face to face with the heart and soul of those ideas, the exemplar of those truths, the inseparable source of the energy that animated the divine system, that was a thought as frightening as it was exhilarating.

The carriage made its way through the stone streets until it finally arrived at the front of 'Abdu'l-Bahá's house. Ali stopped the horse at a walkway which led to a broad flight of steps and a beautiful doorway between two square columns. The grey stone building had dignity, though it was not palatial. To Hasan it seemed massive, regal and forbidding. He looked grimly at Ali and at his elderly mentor, then suddenly he smiled and stepped down.

Before Hasan had taken more than a few steps, there appeared from nowhere a diminutive figure of a man, five feet tall or less. He greeted Hasan and then, as if he had expected this young visitor, guided Hasan toward the door. But before the boy started up the steps, he turned and looked at Moayyed and Ali. He gave a brief nervous gesture with his hand, tried to smile again, but could not, then turned and followed the small man through the front door.

When Hasan emerged from the house that evening, Ali and Moayyed were waiting for him in the carriage. They had no need to ask whether or not everything had gone well — Hasan seemed transformed. His eyes were bright and clear, and he could not stop smiling. He bade farewell to several of the departing believers and walked to the carriage. In his hand was a folded paper which he carried as if it were a royal decree.

He said nothing as he climbed into the back seat of the carriage, but before Ali urged the horse on, Hasan leaned forward and hugged Moayyed. Then he did the same to Ali, though he did not speak. Ali and Moayyed waited impatiently to hear what had happened. Finally, as Ali shook the reins, Hasan announced almost matter-of-factly, 'I am a Bahá'í!'

Ali immediately halted the carriage, and he and Moayyed each took turns embracing Hasan, laughing intermittently.

'Wonderful, wonderful,' mumbled Moayyed. 'Just wonderful.'

When their emotions subsided, Ali guided the carriage through the shadowy streets of Haifa down to the beach road for the hour's journey to 'Akká.

'Perhaps my grandfather can be patient, but I can't,' said Ali. 'Tell us, tell us how it went!'

'Oh, yes, yes,' said Hasan, his hand unconsciously clutching the paper he had not even read. 'He was so . . . so entirely different from anything I expected,' said Hasan, struggling for words that did not exist. 'His eyes, His face, the kindness, I . . .'

Then he looked at Moayyed. 'He knew! Did you tell Him? He already knew!'

'Knew what?' asked Moayyed.

'About Mother and Father! About Yazd and what happened there!'

'Oh, that,' said Moayyed. 'He knows about all those who have given themselves to this Faith; He knows all the names. It's truly amazing.'

'But He knew before I said anything. He welcomed *me* and told the others who *I* was, as if I were important!'

'You *are*,' said Moayyed, taking Hasan's hand and pressing it. 'Your heritage is great. Don't you understand that yet? But tell us more. Tell us the rest!'

'Very well. We entered a room to the left where many believers were already assembled. When I entered, they all turned to me, as if they had been awaiting me.

'I looked around, and at the end of the room was a large empty wicker chair. Then I saw Him! He was seated on the corner of the divan. But He was not dressed in fine robes as I had imagined He would be, nor was His face stern or His voice deep and menacing. He was . . . so kind. He had on a simple 'abá and a low-crowned táj, and when he looked at me, it was as though He had known me for a long, long time and was welcoming me home. Ali, I could literally feel His eyes on me, as though no one had ever really seen me before, not the real me − oh, it's so hard to explain.

'I could not look at Him at first. "Welcome, welcome," I heard Him say, and He motioned for me to sit in the large chair!'

'Did you?' asked Ali.

'I didn't know what else to do − they were all waiting for me. I sat and He asked me to tell Him my name. When I did, He told the others about Mother and Father, who they were and what they had done. In fact, in their honour He told the story of another believer of Yazd, Ḥájí Mullá Mihdíy-i-Yazdí.'

'Ah, yes,' said Moayyed, 'he was the father of the martyr Jináb-i-Varqá. He set out on foot from Yazd, enduring untold pain to reach this place to see Bahá'u'lláh. He reached Mazra'ih, but close by the Mansion he died.'

'Yes,' said Hasan. 'The Master said he is buried at Mazra'ih and that his life symbolizes the power of love.' Hasan paused, lost in his recollection of the meeting.

'And what else?' asked Ali, keeping only half his attention on the carriage.

'What?'

'What else? What's on the paper?'

'The paper? Ah, the paper. I don't know. The man at the door handed it to me as I was leaving!'

'Well, pull up beneath that streetlight before we leave the city and let's see,' said Moayyed, as anxious as the young lads to see what secret the paper contained.

Hasan unfolded the paper and read two verses. The first said, 'A lover feareth nothing and no harm can come nigh him: Thou seest him chill in the fire and dry in the sea.' The other verse said simply, 'Observe My commandments, for the love of My beauty.'

'I believe the first passage is from *The Seven Valleys*,' said Ali.

'Yes, and the second is from the *Aqdas*,' said Moayyed. 'How lovely, how appropriate.'

Hasan gently folded the gift and held it with both hands as if it might fly from him otherwise. He stared at the flickering lights from 'Akká as the carriage crossed onto the beach for the journey home.

The three were silent for a while, physically spent by the events of the long day's journey from Nazareth, but emotionally exhilarated and tranquillized by the propitious outcome of Hasan's visit with the Master.

'When I saw Him,' Hasan said after a while, as though the lull in the conversation had not occurred, 'when I could finally look at Him, I studied His face. It was so beautiful. When He was not talking, the deep lines etched in His brow and around His eyes seemed to be a mask of pain, as if all the sorrows of the world had been known by one man.'

'I think the news of the war affects Him greatly,' said Moayyed.

'But when He talked, all that faded. His eyes seemed to console everyone they looked on. I could not tell their colour − blue or light grey, but it was hard to listen to the words because I wanted so just to watch Him, to see His eyes.

'And there was something else, sir, something amazing to me. With Him in the room, all my questions vanished. My doubts just disappeared. All I could think about was how I might serve Him and the Bahá'í Faith. And my parents,' Hasan continued. 'When He spoke about them, I forgot my sadness, as if they were there being introduced to the other Bahá'ís, as if they were not dead. For the first time I think I understood what they must have felt.'

'What do you mean?' asked Moayyed.

'I can't explain, but I don't think they really suffered. I don't mean they weren't brave. It's just that − well, that feeling of service, you know? That feeling of knowing the value of what you are doing – I think they must have had that kind of . . .'

'Certitude?' Moayyed offered.

'Yes, exactly – *certitude.*'

'I am sure of it,' said Moayyed.

There was silence again. Ali and Moayyed were so aware of the intensity of Hasan's emotions that they spoke little, trying to let the boy share his thoughts and consider the meaning of what he had experienced. They could sense his mind speeding from thought to thought. They knew this was his time, a moment to reflect, a turning-point in his life.

A short while later Hasan blurted out, 'But I don't understand, sir, I really don't understand!'

'Understand what?'

'How could anyone do anything to injure such a one – how could anyone even think of it?' Hasan was referring to the machinations of Mírzá Muḥammad-'Alí, 'Abdu'l-Bahá's half-brother who had rejected the appointment in Bahá'u'lláh's Will of 'Abdu'l-Bahá as Centre of the Covenant and Head of the Faith. More recently, this same brother had been lying to the Ottoman authorities about 'Abdu'l-Bahá, telling them that He was plotting to overthrow the government. In addition to the danger to 'Abdu'l-Bahá's physical person that this sedition caused, the duplicity was taking a greater toll on 'Abdu'l-Bahá in other, more subtle, ways. He had endured this calumny with outward calm and kindness, but He also had to endure the insults of Muḥammad-'Alí and his family whenever he went to visit His Father's tomb at Bahjí where these so-called Covenant-breakers lived in defiance of 'Abdu'l-Bahá's authority and Bahá'u'lláh's explicit instructions to them before His death.

Moayyed had no immediate response to Hasan, and soon Hasan continued. 'It is one thing not to understand who 'Abdu'l-Bahá is when you have never met Him, but they grew up with Him and know what His position is. How can they possibly do such a thing?'

'Who can say?' said Moayyed. 'Perhaps they have lost the fear of God.'

'The *fear* of God? Why should they be afraid of God?'

'Not *afraid* of God,' said Moayyed. 'We should all *fear* God –
there's a difference.'

'I don't understand,' said Hasan.

'Nor I, exactly,' said Ali. 'I've often wondered what it meant – to
fear God.'

'Let me see if I can explain,' said Moayyed. 'Have you ever had a
pet?'

'No, but I had a cousin outside of Yazd who had some horses.'

'Did you ever see him train a young colt?'

'Once, one summer years ago.'

'And how did he do it?'

'He put him on a rope and then had him trot in a circle.'

'And if the horse would not trot correctly?'

'He had a long whip.'

'You mean he beat the horse?'

'No, no. He simply jiggled the whip, and sometimes he would sting
the horse a little.'

'For what reason?'

'To make the horse run correctly.'

'Because, you see, he was teaching the horse respect for his
authority, to show the horse he had a power the horse did not have.
But later, after the horse was more advanced, did he still have the
whip?'

'No. By the summer's end he could whistle and the horse would run
to him.'

'Because he feared him?'

'No, he would reward him with an apple or a bit of sugar.'

'And if he was a good teacher of horses, eventually the horse would
not even need the sugar. You see, once the horse really understood
that the trainer was expressing love, not tyranny, the horse did not
need to perform from fear. But in the beginning, before he knew this,
it was necessary that he understand the power of the trainer.

'But let me give you a better example. When a parent trains a child,
he or she gives the child rules, laws. The parent then admonishes the

child to obey, even though the child does not understand the reason for the rules, correct?'

'I suppose.'

'Well, if you had a child, and the child were playing near a nest of hornets, what would you do?'

'I would tell the child to stay away from the nest, naturally,' said Hasan.

'And if it would not?'

'I would scold it.'

'And if it still refused to obey?'

'I would restrain it somehow, keep it from danger.'

'But the child would probably not understand your scolding and your restraint, would it? It might perceive you as being cruel.'

'Nevertheless, I would have to protect the child.'

'Then protection would be more important to you at the time than whether or not the child understood your reasoning or the love you were really expressing?'

'Yes.'

'That is how mankind is trained as well. Many, many times Bahá'u'lláh says that the trainer of mankind is reward and punishment. These He calls the pillars of justice.'

'But God doesn't have a whip. I know that in the Old Testament stories God punishes the tribes when they do wrong, but those are just stories, aren't they — God doesn't speak from the sky and cause earthquakes and things, does He?'

Moayyed looked through the darkness down the beach to the city of 'Akká before them. The waves from the Mediterranean drummed a hypnotic rhythm as the carriage wheels crunched through the hard-packed sand.

'Let's do this,' said Moayyed, 'let's pretend that you and Ali are high up on a building, for instance in the tower of the muezzin in the Mosque of Jazzár Páshá.' Both boys looked to 'Akká and could barely make out in the night sky the slender spire above the mosque. 'Suddenly, Ali begins to climb out onto the ledge and dance.' Ali laughed and shook his head at his grandfather's quaint imagination.

'You may laugh now,' said Moayyed to Ali, 'but you did some things almost that dangerous — in your younger days, of course.' Then turning to Hasan he asked, 'Now, what would you do?'

'I would tell him to stop!'

'And if he did not?'

'I would warn him that he might get hurt if he didn't stop.'

'And if he did not stop, if he fell, what would be the result?'

'What?' asked Hasan. 'If he fell? Why, he would be killed, or at least horribly injured.'

'Would you call that his punishment — because he didn't obey you?'

'Punishment? No, of course not. It was an accident.'

'An accident that occurred because he did not obey you.'

'Yes, but *I* did not cause him to be injured — I did not punish him myself.'

'Then what did?'

'Gravity,' said Ali, with a laugh.

'That's true!' said Moayyed, in perfect seriousness. 'The very law which Hasan's admonition was warning you about — that was the force which punished you.'

'It seems to me that it isn't the law's fault,' said Hasan. 'It seems to me that he punished himself on the law. I wouldn't blame a wall if I ran into it.'

'Quite so,' said Moayyed. 'That's the proper way to say it, isn't it? In fact, Bahá'u'lláh says much the same thing about those who reject the guidance God sends through His Prophets: "He who shall accept and believe, shall receive his reward; and he who shall turn away, shall receive none other than his own punishment."'

'And is that what the Old Testament stories portray?' asked Hasan.

'Precisely,' said Moayyed. 'The laws of God, like the laws of nature, work whether we obey them or not. If we disobey them, we suffer the consequences, not because God is cruel or vengeful, but because the laws are always operating.'

'Then why isn't it explained that clearly in the Old Testament? Why did they believe things happened because God was angry or sad or jealous?'

'Because when we are young and unsophisticated, as were the tribes described in those stories, we cannot understand the way laws operate. Like young children, like the young colt your cousin used to train, we can only understand authority, or reward and punishment. That's why in the beginning the child looks upon the parents' laws as a prison, as the expression of restriction, when in reality the wise parent gives guidance and rules as an expression of love, just as God does through His Manifestations.'

'Guides through the junkroom,' said Ali.

'Then why should we *fear* God?' asked Hasan.

'What we fear is the consequence of our disobedience because we come to understand that to disobey is to cause harm to ourselves since God's laws and guidance are devised totally for our assistance and well-being.'

'Because He is really trying to protect us?'

'From our own unfortunate behaviour?'

'Like dancing on a minaret?' said Ali.

'Or sailing too far past the sea wall,' said Moayyed.

There was a brief silence again. Hasan recalled once more the face of 'Abdu'l-Bahá, the absolute kindness and power emanating from those clear eyes. It still did not make sense to him and he said so.

'But they *know* Him; they *see* Him. Some have watched Him all their lives, and yet they turn away? How can that be? Are they simply evil?'

'No one is *simply* evil, Hasan. Never think such a thing. Evil is hardly simple, that is why it is so frightening. Who knows why the Covenant-breakers create such mischief. To know that you would have to know their hearts. Only God knows that. We cannot really know them or judge them. We can only learn from them that even the near ones can fail.'

'Perhaps it is because they are too close,' said Ali.

'It could very well be. Having grown up with 'Abdu'l-Bahá, they might be tempted to think, ''He is only my brother – perhaps I am as eloquent as He.'' I know that is what happened with Fareed and Khayru'lláh. They would teach the message of Bahá'u'lláh, and because of its incredible power to transform the lives of those who hear it, they began to be amazed at the effect they were having and the control they could wield. They probably began to believe that this power and authority came from themselves, instead of from 'Abdu'l-Bahá who had sent them and guided them in the first place.'

'And what happened to them,' asked Hasan.

'They fell from the minaret,' said Ali.

'More or less,' said Moayyed. 'The same thing that happened to Mírzá Yahyá before them — like branches presuming to live apart from the tree, they withered. They were left without followers or influence of any sort, and bereft of the joy they once had in serving.'

'Does that mean they are condemned forever?' asked Hasan. 'Are all the good things they did simply lost?'

'What do *you* think?' asked Moayyed. 'Do you think they should be damned forever and that all the sincerely good actions they did before are worthless?'

'Not really.'

'Do you think God less fair or just or forgiving than you?'

'No,' said Hasan, with a broad grin.

'Indeed not.'

'I have heard some Bahá'ís say that they could see the beginnings of defection in the Covenant-breakers before they rebelled,' said Ali.

'Perhaps they saw characteristics that later lent themselves to such action,' said Moayyed, 'but who does not have such flaws? No, I do not think that the Covenant-breakers are innately evil or doomed. Remember, Bahá'u'lláh in the *Aqdas* told Mírzá Yahyá that even he — one who had tried to murder the Manifestation of God — even he would be forgiven if he would but repent. Remember also that someone as devoted as Nabíl once rebelled, then renounced his actions and spent the rest of his life in devoted service.'

'Then they are not evil?' asked Ali.

'Nothing is evil of itself,' said Moayyed. 'God gives us freedom to choose and we can choose wrongly. If we respect God's law, if we are constantly aware that His laws are for our protection, then we fear to do aught but good, because we do not want to injure ourselves. The more wrong choices we make, the further we get from understanding.

'Let me put it this way. In a darksome night you might set a lantern in a tree to do your work. And if you turned away from the lantern, you might not see as well. You could turn back toward the light and see again. But if you wandered so far away from the lantern that you could no longer detect its light, you might not be able to make it back on your own — you might be lost in the darkness. That is the fear you should have, the fear of losing your way in the night.'

'Then it is not God we fear, but ourselves,' said Hasan. He then felt the paper in his hands. It was too dark to see the writing, but he remembered the verse: 'A lover feareth nothing and no harm can come nigh him: Thou seest him chill in the fire and dry in the sea.' Mentally he recalled feature by feature the face of 'Abdu'l-Bahá as the lights from 'Akká grew brighter and the three tired figures returned home.

14

The Light that Shines in Darkness

THE next two weeks were heaven on earth for Hasan. There were gatherings in his honour, gifts from people he had never even met. How curious it all seemed to him, to bear the name 'Bahá'í' as a badge of honour, as a cause for celebration, when in Yazd the same name had been a reason for children to chide or ridicule him. He had often cringed when a fellow student discovered his parents had been 'Bábís', as the townspeople referred to all Bahá'ís.

That fear was largely gone now. He still did not understand the events that had led to his parents' death nor had he resolved the deep anger he felt toward their persecutors. He could not understand the mentality of those who would in the name of religion torture and slaughter innocent, God-fearing people. Or if on some intellectual level he understood, he could not forgive. That residual anger was the seed of a darkness that began to germinate in Hasan.

At first Hasan mentioned none of this. He was hesitant to ask questions now that he himself was a Bahá'í. After all, the Bahá'í Faith was now *his* religion and he supposed he should be responsible for his own spiritual dilemmas. He could not even tell Ali, whom he loved as a brother, or Aunt Nahid and Uncle Husayn, who were now becoming like mother and father to him. It was not that he doubted their capacity to understand; rather he felt guilty, as if he were being hypocritical. After all, he had accepted the teachings of the Bahá'í Faith, and yet he still had questions. Had he been premature in his decision? Had he let the emotions of the moment override his better judgement?

At first he was only vaguely aware of these thoughts. He enjoyed the companionship of Ali. He began to become familiar with the maze-like streets of 'Akká as he and his cousin explored all the secrets contained within 'Akká's ancient walls. He prayed dutifully, helped out in whatever way he could, made many new friends among the other Bahá'í youth in the settlement. But over the weeks, the suppressed resentment grew in him, and near the end of June two things happened that significantly altered his determination to keep these feelings to himself.

The first of these occurred one afternoon when he went with the Mashhadis to visit the Shrine of Bahá'u'lláh at Bahjí. It was his first opportunity to see this most sanctified spot, the Qiblih, the Point of Adoration for Bahá'ís around the world. As they passed by the outer residences of the sprawling mansion, Hasan was shocked that some of the Covenant-breakers, the family of Mírzá Muḥammad-'Alí, were taunting the pilgrims and denouncing the name of 'Abdu'l-Bahá.

None of the Bahá'ís said a word. None even looked in their direction, except Hasan who saw them standing at the balcony railings shaking their fists in defiant gestures. Suddenly he was struck with the reality of evil – not a faceless abstraction as in his dreams, but living, motivated human personalities, quite purposefully screaming indignities against the face of God on earth, ranting in the secret pain of their inner darkness against the signs of light.

These were not passive acts of rejection, not some accident of a misguided soul making an unfortunate choice. This was evil – active, forceful, mischievous and conscious evil. These people, like those who had tortured and killed his parents, had not simply turned away from light – surely they turned toward something powerful and frightening. How else could the eternal plan of God become so perverted through the centuries?

That thought, obvious as it was profound, struck Hasan forcefully – how *could* the plan of an All-Powerful Being become perverted? If God be just, kind and loving, then why was not the world He created a reflection of that same benignity? It hardly seemed sufficient to acknowledge that mankind had been created free to choose and that some chose poorly.

Such a ponderous question did not occur at once, but grew slowly over succeeding days and weeks. It became crystallized in Hasan's mind one day when he visited the barracks with Ali, or at least as close to the barracks as they could get without risking the disfavour of the Ottoman officials. As they examined the spot where Bahá'u'lláh and over seventy other Bahá'ís were cruelly imprisoned, Hasan further realized the wilfulness of persecution and fanaticism. The towns-people, the guards, they knew exactly what they were doing. They may not have known the intricacies of the teachings of these Persian exiles, but surely they could have seen that the Bahá'ís meant no harm to anyone.

It was that evening that Hasan decided to ask his aunt about the details of his parents' death, something he had never asked his grandmother because she refused to talk about the matter in any way whatsoever. Because she felt it was time for Hasan to know, to realize his parents' courage and to know his own heritage, Nahid spelled out the details as she had learned them from Sadiq and other Bahá'ís from Yazd.

She tried to remain calm as she spoke of beatings, of their flesh slashed, of their being set on fire while the living flesh yet ran with blood, but she could not. She maintained her role as parent for a few minutes, then dissolved in sorrow in recollection of her sister's sweet frame so desecrated. Hasan did not cry – not then. To him his parents were still shadowy figures, and the events were the abstract impressions that he might have got from one of the adventure stories he loved so dearly. But later that same evening, alone in his room, the images became clear to him, as did his longing for his parents' love. The walls inside him, carefully built over the years of protecting himself from just such thoughts, came crashing down. Inside a flood of anger, passion, grief and guilt swirled together and dragged him down.

He slept little that night, but when the room gradually began to become visible in the light of the morning, Hasan felt a little healed, as if some of the bitter gall had been drained from his poisoned spirit. And yet he was hardly soothed or refreshed. In the place of the hardness, the sealed up part of him, was the question, unrelenting and implacable — if God created a good world, what was the source of such iniquity?

Then, just after he had said a dawn prayer, he recalled something Khanum had said to him the day she had consoled him about Tela. 'Let questions be your friends,' she had said. 'Let them guide you on the true path. If you hide them away, they will become like termites and will eat at the foundation of your happy home.'

Hasan immediately determined what he must do. With Nahid's permission, he went to see Moayyed. Without so much as a hint as to what was going on, Hasan took Moayyed to a place on the city walls that overlooked the crashing waves of the Mediterranean sea and the barracks where Bahá'u'lláh had been imprisoned. He helped the old man up the few steps and they sat down.

It was a beautiful spot, even amid the crowded squalor of 'Akká. In the distance Carmel called out. Before them could be clearly seen the window to the cell where a Manifestation of God had been imprisoned by the Muslim authorities. Behind those buildings, outside the busy streets of 'Akká, lay the countryside and Bahjí, Mazra'ih, the Riḍván Gardens.

Moayyed could tell something was bothering his protégé, but he could sense that the boy in his purposefulness would soon disclose what was on his mind.

Hasan wasted no time in explaining why he had brought Moayyed to this particular spot. Pointing to the barracks, Hasan said, 'When the officials brought the Bahá'ís here, when they read the farmán to the people, they expected the Bahá'ís to die, didn't they?'

'Yes,' said Moayyed, 'yes, I suppose they did.'

'You remember on the ride back from Haifa that night when you talked to me about the Covenant-breakers — you explained to me why they deny 'Abdu'l-Bahá?'

'I gave you some suggestions, that's true?'

'You said we should not judge them, didn't you?'

'True.'

'Yet we should not associate with them.'

'For our own protection — that's correct.'

'Sir, those who put Bahá'u'lláh in prison, and those who injure others and know exactly what they are doing — '

'Such as those who murdered your parents?'

'Yes, sir,' said Hasan, in a softer tone. 'Like them. How do you explain them? Do you really think they simply turned away from the light of truth?'

'I take it that you do not find this a satisfying explanation,' said Moayyed, trying with all his might to discern the troubled thoughts of the boy. 'Is this a question or an accusation?'

'Sir?'

'Some questions we ask to discover answers — others are like arrows we use to attack our prey. They are rhetorical questions, questions that really conceal an accusation. Aren't you really asking how such things can occur if God is in control of things?' He touched Hasan's arm as he spoke. It was a simple gesture, but it had a profound effect on the boy, as if to signal to Hasan that here was not his enemy, but a loving friend to help him with his struggle.

With that Hasan opened up to Moayyed. He told him the haunting question that had grown within him over the past weeks. He repeated the details of his parents' death that Nahid had shared with him the night before. Then he referred back to the Covenant-breakers and the shock of seeing their faces and watching them mock the visitors to the Shrine.

'In their eyes was a power, and it frightened me to think that God could allow it to exist. You say they are blinded by the light or look upon the Manifestation or 'Abdu'l-Bahá simply as men. But they must know they are hurting others. Or the rulers who send so many to their deaths in these wars, surely they know the evil that they do.

Don't you think people know when they are doing wrong?'

Moayyed looked up at the sky. It was clear, a vivid blue, and gulls played in the sea breeze like children on the beach. Then he looked at Hasan straight on. His hazel eyes that had seen so much in one lifetime were suddenly more powerful than Hasan had ever seen them. He spoke, and though there was love in his heart, the tone of his voice was factual and severe.

'Of course I do. Each of us, each and every one of us has a power, Hasan, a power to accomplish untold good or unthinkable evil. Certainly we can do evil while knowing it is wrong. Why, any one of us can so condition ourselves to perpetrate the most dreadful and inhumane of acts without feeling the least bit of remorse in this life. That is a terrifying reality, that we can become so debased; but it is the truth, and yet it is only one part of the truth.'

'I don't understand,' said Hasan, meekly.

Moayyed put his hand to his forehead and rubbed twice, took a deep breath and looked at the barracks window. 'Hasan, if I were to send you right now to the Arctic, to the North Pole, what would happen?'

'Sir?'

'If you were to travel as far north as north can be, what would happen to you?'

'I guess I would freeze to death in the ice and snow.'

'Then the cold of the Arctic would destroy you?'

'Yes.'

'Tell me, then, what is the source of coldness?'

'I don't understand.'

'What force in this world causes coldness?'

Hasan thought. There were the icy winds and snow, and yet they were effects of cold, not causes. Then he remembered from his classes how in the winter season the earth tilts so that the sun shines less directly. And at the North Pole or the South Pole, there was never much direct light.

'There is no source of coldness,' he said at last; 'there is only the absence of light and heat.'

'And darkness,' asked Moayyed, 'is that not the same?'

'Yes,' said Hasan. 'I suppose that's true. There is no source of darkness except the absence of light.'

'Yet both conditions, darkness and cold, they can have a profound effect on you, can they not?'

'Certainly!' Hasan admitted.

'Both have all the properties of energy.'

'What do you mean by that, sir?'

'These conditions, they are both an absence of energy, yet like energy itself, they cause amazing changes. They can have profound effects on our lives, on our planet, just as energy does.'

'I see what you mean – yes, they do.'

Moayyed again put his hand on Ali's forearm and spoke once more with a commanding tone. 'Evil is the same, Hasan. There is no source of evil, no being in the universe perpetrating evil, sending out evil emissaries to infect others. Evil occurs whenever we reject godliness, whenever someone turns away from the light of divine guidance. But remember this, each choice, each action has results, significant and lasting results.' He looked over toward Mt Carmel – in his mind's eye he saw the Shrine of the Báb and the House of 'Abdu'l-Bahá. 'Why, if I were to reject the Bahá'í principles in my life . . .' He did not complete the thought. He didn't need to.

'You could never become . . .'

'Evil?' said Moayyed.

'Well, I wasn't going to say . . .'

'Say it, for evil it would be. By all means, we must use powerful and dramatic words to describe these dreadful conditions. At the North Pole would you say to me, "Moayyed, the absence of heat is taking my life!"'

'No, sir,' said Hasan, with a smile.

'Indeed you would not. "Help! Moayyed!" you would call. "The freezing wind and snow are numbing my hands and feet! Help me, or the cold will destroy me!"'

'I think you are right,' said Hasan, with a chuckle.

'But do you understand my point, Hasan? Evil may be the absence of goodness, but that is a powerful condition.'

'Is all evil the absence of goodness?' asked Hasan.

'All of it.'

'What about earthquakes?' asked Hasan.

'You don't make anything easy, do you?' said Moayyed, patting Hasan on the shoulder. 'Hasan, not all things we perceive as unfortunate can be said to be *evil*. The term *evil* we reserve for those things determined by human choice. No one chooses whether or not there will be an earthquake. It is an accident of nature. It is true we can learn vital lessons from such accidents, painful though they be. But such events are not evil in the sense that they don't involve human tyranny or injustice.'

'But they are still evil, are they not? They kill people.'

'They certainly test the families of those who die, and certainly they cause sorrow, but such testing is not necessarily bad.'

'Isn't it bad for the ones who die?'

'Through no fault of their own they have left this plane of existence and have begun their lives in the next world, something every individual must eventually do. Furthermore, you can be sure that a loving and merciful God assists them in the transition to that new existence so that they suffer no injustice because of their untimely departure.'

Hasan listened and tried to relate Moayyed's observations to his own situation, he who had been left behind. 'It still doesn't seem fair,' said Hasan, 'not for those who now must live without their friends or family.'

Moayyed sensed now the heart and soul of Hasan's dilemma, but he knew no easy way to respond to the boy's pain. 'Son, what exactly do you think is the purpose of this life?'

'Bahá'u'lláh says it is to know and to worship God.'

'But tell me, in your own words, what you think.'

'To learn, to learn about things, to learn about people and the world, and ... I don't know, to make the world better somehow.'

'And what is your part in this? What do you think is your special task?'

'I suppose to be the best Hasan I can be.'

'And what do you think causes Hasan to become better, to grow, to mature, to become the very best Hasan that can possibly be?'

'I'm not sure,' said Hasan. 'Just trying, I guess.' He thought about the changes that had occurred in him during the past six months. He recalled what life had been like before he had come to 'Akká. What had changed him? What had enabled him to become stronger and surer?

'Let me put it this way,' said Moayyed. 'You see the boys swimming in the bay?' Far off in the distance there were several figures splashing in the water near where some fishermen were trawling their nets.

'Yes, I see them.'

'If I wanted to teach you to swim, what would I need to do?'

'Put me in the water,' said Hasan, thinking to make a joke.

'True!' said Moayyed, to Hasan's surprise. 'And would you enjoy that experience?'

'Not if I didn't know how to swim.'

'And if I succeeded in teaching you and you overcame that test, if I wanted to make you a great swimmer, a champion, should I begin to give you lectures about swimming, or something else?'

'You would have to make me swim all the time.'

'Wouldn't that be simple?'

'It would be very hard until my body was conditioned to the strain, but what are you trying to say?'

'We learn by tests, by struggling against our present limitations, do we not? We learn by having to do more than we know how to do at the moment. Why, if you simply went into the water and never exerted yourself, never pushed yourself beyond your limits, you could only be as good as you are now, correct?'

'That's true enough.'

'It's the same way in school. If your teacher wants to help you progress, your tests must become more and more difficult so that the teacher can measure your increased knowledge.'

'Yes.'

'It is the same with this life, Hasan. We are always changing. We may be getting stronger or weaker, but we are always changing. So it is that the Bahá'í writings teach us that without tests, without struggle, without increased exertion, there is no progress. All of the accidents of this life, everything we think of as unfortunate, has the ability to stretch us, to force us to grow and develop. In fact, without such tests, we could never go beyond where we are.'

'You mean that all such things are sent by God?'

'No. But since we cannot know which are and which are not, we would do well to assume that they all have a divine purpose and then they will.'

Hasan considered Moayyed's advice. It sounded good, and yet Hasan recalled how many people suffered who, to him, seemed to have already learned what they needed to know. He thought of Khanum, her body racked with disease. He thought of those maimed from the daily horrors of warfare.

'But what about the people who are already good?' said Hasan. 'Even if the innocent are cared for in the next life, what about those who remain behind and are good? Why are they tested?'

'Think again about your swimming, Hasan. I am your coach and I have you in tip-top training — you are in peak condition and ready to win. Should I now stop your training?'

'Of course not,' said Hasan.

'In fact, that would be cruel, would it not?'

'I suppose so.'

'Of course it would be, to have you come so far, only to let your stamina and hard-won expertise dwindle into a memory. No, if anyone needs to be tested, it is those who are most prepared. Remember, Bahá'u'lláh has stated that no one is tested beyond his or her capacity. Well, the capacity of the spiritually élite is greater than the rest, and so to the rest of us their misery seems unbearable.' Moayyed paused and looked at Hasan kindly. 'To put it simply, Hasan, a test is not a test unless it tests us. Our purpose here is to be trained, to be taught and prepared, not to become as comfortable as we possibly can, though certainly the moments of peace and tranquillity have something to teach us as well.'

Hasan looked again at the barracks window. 'Sir, do you think evil people — or rather people who do evil things — do you think they really know that what they are doing is wrong?'

'Yes, on some level they know. I believe that, but I will leave that between them and God.'

'But why would someone do something he knows will hurt him? Don't you think if people really knew they were injuring their own souls they would not do such things?'

'Hasan, have you never done something even though you knew in your heart it was wrong, even though you suspected you would have to suffer the consequences of what you did?'

'Like what?' said Hasan, nervously.

'Oh, eating too much candy, for example. You knew it was bad for you. You knew it would upset your stomach — you might have even suspected you would be punished, and yet you decided the immediate satisfaction was more important than any future consequences, so you did it anyway.'

'Yes, that's true.'

'And worse things, possibly?' Moayyed's knowing look required no answer. 'You see, our choices as people are not so simple as following the dictates of our logical minds.'

'What do you mean?'

'We are not machines, my boy. We are not machines. Our brains have the ability to assimilate information, to show us our choices, but we also have what 'Abdu'l-Bahá calls a mighty will, the force that makes the choice itself. That power comes from our souls and it is affected by a thousand things — our desires, our character, our selfishness, forces we can only guess at. But in those crucial moments, in those times when our destiny is balanced on our own will, that is when our mettle is tested, those are the times when we determine whether we shall progress and develop or become less than we are. And you know something else? These moments occur all the time, every day.'

'I know they do,' said Hasan.

'Well, do you forgive God now?' asked Moayyed.

'Forgive God? What do you mean?'

'It seems to me a few minutes ago you were ready to accuse God of creating a very unjust universe.'

'Not unjust, just hard for me to understand sometimes.'

'You mean,' said Moayyed, using a cane to struggle to his feet, 'you mean it tests you?'

'Yes, sir,' said Hasan, reaching out to help the loved patriarch, 'it does indeed.'

15

The Children of Riḍván

FOR the next several days Hasan kept to himself. At first his Aunt Nahid feared he was again becoming the sombre spirit he had been at his arrival. But when she inquired, discreetly so as not to embarrass him, he told her that he was fine.

'I just need to think about some things.'

His smile reassured her, but being his foster-mother, she could not help worrying a little about him. She thought of asking Ali to approach Hasan, but decided Hasan might think she was meddling. Besides, Hasan seemed to enjoy being by himself. He had grown up with no brothers or sisters and few playmates, so being alone was nothing new to him.

Hasan felt extremely close to Ali, to Aunt Nahid and Uncle Husayn, but it had been a while since he had been able to go off by himself, and he was still mulling over Moayyed's conversation about evil, trying as hard as he could to accept the events surrounding his parents' death.

Some of his confusion had been resolved. When he had come to 'Akká, he was unable even to think about what had happened to them, let alone talk to someone else about his vague recollection of that gruesome night. Now he found himself thinking about his parents constantly, trying to understand how such a thing could occur. In the Bahá'í scriptures he would read about the glorious destiny of mankind, about the bounties of living in 'this Day', the very time the Prophets of old had longed to witness, the fulfilment of human promise.

If on some level he could believe Moayyed's explanation about how evil occurs, he could not yet forgive, and that troubled him most of all, as if to forgive the malefactors was to betray his parents. And it was more than their memory he wished to safeguard − if he understood correctly the role of the Bahá'ís, it was to ensure as much as possible the implementation of divine principles, to assist and reward the righteous and punish the wicked. To forgive them, to let them go, even in his thoughts, seemed to be a violation of that trust.

For two days Hasan went to 'Ali's hill', as he referred to Tall i-Fakhkhar, the ancient mound outside the town walls that overlooked the seashore and 'Akká itself. Months before, Ali had told Hasan in detail of the dream he had once had there, how it had initiated a very special period in his own quest to understand his identity as a Bahá'í. Hasan thought that if the hill had played such a mystical part in Ali's search, it might have the same effect on him.

For more than an hour he sat there, enjoying the beautiful view of the mountains, the sea, and the towns of Haifa and 'Akká facing each other across the bay. He tried to grapple with these thoughts, believing that if he could resolve these feelings satisfactorily, if he could think about his parents without feeling guilt or anger or despair, he would be free to approach their memory without fear and he would be reconciled with his beliefs as a Bahá'í.

But in spite of Moayyed's explanation about how evil takes place, and even though Hasan no longer had nightmares, he felt unworthy, guilty, as if he were unqualified to bear the appellation 'Bahá'í' until he could let go of this anger and desire for vengeance. Try as he might, Hasan did not feel detached, not from his anger and indignation. And the longer these thoughts persisted and interfered with his enjoyment of his beliefs, the more determined he became to resolve the matter. He could accept Moayyed's assurance that there was no demonic force in the universe, no Satan bent on undermining God's creation.

But did that make a difference? After all, he thought, what did it matter what caused people to do wrong — it was the actions that counted, wasn't it?

By the second day of brooding over these perplexing questions, Hasan found that instead of extricating himself from his negative feelings, his thoughts were becoming circular; he was becoming ever more deeply embroiled in his emotions, 'stewing in his own juices', as his grandmother had said.

Toward the early afternoon of the second day, he found the hilltop perch no longer peaceful or comforting. He stood up, stretched, then descended the hill and began walking instinctively toward the Qiblih at Bahjí, drawn as if by a magnet toward that source of inspiration. As he was passing by the Riḍván Gardens, he decided to stop and escape temporarily the hot sun and perhaps to take a tangerine or two from the garden's well-tended fruit trees.

He walked beneath the stone arch over the small footbridge and seated himself beneath the shade of spreading mulberry trees. A steady breeze wafted among the flowers and plants on the small island, intermingling the various fragrances into one subtle but entrancing aroma, as if all the spiritual energy released by the many visits of Bahá'u'lláh and 'Abdu'l-Bahá to this spot had been transformed into a divine perfume.

Because the air was dry this first week in July, the heat was a little more bearable; the wind was almost cool in the shade. Hasan sat on one of the old wooden benches and looked out across the fields that shone so brightly through the leafy branches of the garden trees. He pulled from his pocket a piece of paper on which he had penned a passage from the writings of Bahá'u'lláh. It was a passage from *The Book of Certitude*, a portion called the 'Tablet of the True Seeker'. In exquisite language, the Prophet had portrayed in some detail the attributes all people of religious conviction should aspire to.

From that lengthy exposition, Hasan had copied the following verses: 'He should not wish for others that which he doth not wish for himself ... He should forgive the sinful, and never despise his low estate, for none knoweth what his own end shall be.'

The paper was thoroughly wrinkled from having been repeatedly taken out and folded again. Hasan read it once more, then looked across the garden path at the bench on which the Author of those same words was wont to sit on afternoons such as this. But proximity to this sacred spot only increased in Hasan his sense of guilt, his feeling of unworthiness. Some of the sinful he could forgive, but not murderers who had deprived him of mother and father, of happiness, of sleep.

Echoing in his brain like the refrain from a child's song was a passage from *The Hidden Words* he had heard only once before: 'Hast thou ever heard that friend and foe should abide in one heart? Cast out then the stranger, that the Friend may enter His home.'

Hasan knew that his venomous thoughts – this anger, this need for vengeance – these were his foes. So long as they dwelled within, they would drive out the friend. It was not that he *wanted* to feel these things – he would happily relinquish the hatred if he knew how. This very morning before he had walked to Tall i-Fakhkhar he had prayed as sincerely as he knew how the *Tablet of Aḥmad* that he might be released from these furies. He sat quietly, trying to let go. He concentrated on the scented breeze, the chirping songbirds, the rippling water from stream and fountain. Within minutes he fell into a shallow half-sleep. How long he remained in that state of balance he knew not, but the next thing he became aware of was an approaching sound, dream-like.

There were no footsteps, yet there was a presence. With effort he opened his eyes, turned and saw the outline of a figure – a woman, a girl? He could not tell. His eyes were not adjusted to the light, and the afternoon sunlight glared behind her. She was not standing, yet she was moving toward him, her head covered in a white lace shawl.

'I see you had the same idea,' said a voice so soft and melodious that Hasan could only suppose he was yet sleeping or dreaming as the figure floated before him. 'What is your name?' it said.

'Hasan,' he answered, 'Hasan-'Alí Yazdí.'

'I have cousins in Yazd,' said a young, feminine voice as the figure moved out of the glare and Hasan could see more clearly. It was not a dream or spirit. It was a young woman, her face smiling brightly, her eyes dark and large, her cheeks dimpled, her lips full. Her face was a mask of confidence and strength even though, as Hasan was shocked to see, she was confined to a wheelchair.

'I am Rezvani,' she said, 'Rezvani Bushrú'í.'

'Are you related to Mr Badí‘ Bushrú'í, the teacher?' asked Hasan. 'Distant relatives,' she said.

'I am the first cousin of Ali Mashhadi,' said Hasan.

'I thought you might be,' said Rezvani. 'I saw you here once before. My father is a gardener here and helps Abu'l-Qásim.'

Hasan watched her intently as she spoke, especially her eyes. He could not tell her age. She appeared to be sixteen or seventeen, but in her speech she seemed much older and Hasan did not know how to address her.

'I have been here only once before,' he said.

'I'm sorry if I interrupted your meditation. I come here every afternoon about this time.' She looked out across the fields and Hasan studied her face. As inconspicuously as he could, he observed her delicate hands that gripped the rims of the wheels.

'I was almost asleep,' said Hasan with an embarrassed laugh.

'I see,' she said with a glance so powerful, so penetrating, that Hasan had to avert his eyes.

'You appear to be young,' she said, 'yet you talk like someone much older. You must have suffered in your life.' Hasan did not respond. 'I am sixteen years old,' she offered, as if to allow Hasan to identify himself further.

'I am almost fourteen,' he said, and then, 'I just became a Bahá'í.' It was a *non sequitur*, but somehow it seemed appropriate, as if it explained everything important about himself − this is what I am; this is where I am going in my life's journey.

'Really?' she said. 'How exciting for you!' Her tone did not imply the obvious question − why are you only now becoming a Bahá'í if you are Ali's cousin. 'I know your parents must be pleased.'

'They are dead,' Hasan said for the first time in his life, almost matter-of-factly, almost angrily.

'I am sorry,' she said without a trace of discomfort. 'Nevertheless, I am sure they rejoice.'

Her confidence was infectious. Hasan might have resented the comment from someone else — how could anyone presume that all was well with his mother and father? How could anyone take so calmly and casually what had wrecked his life. But such was not the case with Rezvani.

'Perhaps so,' Hasan conceded, though the tone of his response made it clear that he himself had no such assurance, or if he did, it was hardly sufficient recompense. 'Did you get your name from the garden?' he asked, trying to change the subject.

'No,' laughed Rezvani, 'though I might as well have; I am here so often. We have been here only a year. We came here from Búshihr where my father was a merchant.'

Rezvani went on to explain how during renewed agitation against the local Bahá'ís, villagers ransacked their shop and burned all their possessions, how she had been permanently injured when a beam collapsed on her back, how her mother had perished in the fire.

'Father was out of the village that day, and I lay there powerless to rescue my mother's unconscious body from the flames. Of course, the villagers would not lift a finger.' Her voice was calm and resigned, but she suddenly looked away for a moment before she could continue.

'My father decided he could no longer live among such people and we travelled here. It took many months.'

Hasan had no response and fumbled for something to say. He felt uncomfortable, as if her confidence and resilience was an indictment of his own emotions. Finally she herself stated blankly the bare truth of his heart.

'You seem to be preoccupied,' she said; 'are you sad about your parents?'

The question took Hasan by surprise, and yet who had a better right than she to make such an observation?

'It has been many years,' Hasan answered, as if to apologize for his grief, 'almost ten.' How could she understand that he was only now coming to face the reality of their deaths, that for him the disaster was only now becoming something he could talk about?

'Do you feel responsible?' asked Rezvani.

'What?' asked Hasan, trying to decipher what she meant — how could a three-year-old child be responsible for the murder of his parents, and yet the question had a familiar feeling to it.

'For several months after my mother died, I felt an overpowering guilt,' Rezvani continued, 'as if I were responsible for her death. I talked with my father, but he was too grief-stricken to help much. But my grandmother, she understood perfectly. She helped me realize that the event had so shattered my life that my emotions were confused. I was feeling angry because of my legs, then guilty because I was more concerned about my legs than I was about mother, then angry at father because he was so shocked by mother's death that he could do nothing to console me.' She paused again. 'It was a difficult time.'

'And now?' asked Hasan.

'Now,' said Rezvani with a sudden vigour and bright smile, 'now life is good. Father and I are very close. He is still scarred, I fear, but he is a good man, a kind man. We help each other from day to day.'

'Don't you wish you could do something to the people who did this to you? Don't you wish justice could be done?'

'Justice will be done, Hasan. In truth I feel sorry for the villagers. Some came to me later in tears to apologize. Others were simply doing what the mullas had told them was right, to rid the Muslim Faith of those they believe to be infidels.'

'And the rest? What of those who knew that they were doing wrong?'

'I don't know who they are, Hasan. If you were to line them all up, I could not say who knew and who did not. Could you? I do know that all of them must eventually face the consequences of what they have done. You know that as well as I.'

'Not in this life.'

'Perhaps not, but I think I can accept that. If I can believe that mother is being treated with love in the spiritual realm, I can certainly believe that those responsible for her death will receive justice there.'

'That's true, isn't it?' said Hasan. 'If our parents are treated fairly, then everyone else will be too.'

'That's what justice means to me,' said Rezvani, 'fairness, what is fair and appropriate.'

'And is it fair that I forget what I feel about the ones who killed my own parents? Put aside my obligation to see that justice is done? Doesn't Bahá'u'lláh say that the most precious thing is justice?'

'If there is anything you can do to see that they receive justice in this life, then do it! Is there? Is there anything at all you can do?'

'Not really,' Hasan admitted, as he looked down to the earth. 'Nothing that matters.'

'Then what is justice for you? What is appropriate for you?'

'That's the problem. I don't know. What do you think?'

'To let go of those feelings.'

'To be "detached",' said Hasan, filling in the appropriate word.

'Yes,' said Rezvani. 'Does that bother you? Do you feel it would be wrong to let go, to leave their judgement to God?'

'In a way,' Hasan admitted.

'Then respond to your reason and not to your emotions,' said Rezvani. 'That's one of the meanings of "detachment" as far as I am concerned, to let go of your emotions once they have delivered the message.'

'What message?' asked Hasan. 'What do you mean?'

'Do you know the story of Badí'?' asked Rezvani.

'I know that he delivered a letter from Bahá'u'lláh to the Shah and was killed for it.'

'That's right; what's more, he knew he would be. At least, Bahá'u'lláh warned him that he might well be killed, because the letter was not something the Shah would want to hear. Now, see how foolish the Shah was, to kill the messenger because he brought a painful message?'

'Yes, but what does that have to do with emotions?'

'Emotions are simply messengers. They tell us how we are doing. You accomplish some difficult task, you feel proud. You do poorly, you feel disappointed in yourself. If you do not live up to your expectations of yourself, then you feel guilty.

'I have thought about this a great deal during the past two years because I had to deal with the exact same problem. Emotions are subtle and tricky.'

'What did you learn from all that thinking?' asked Hasan.

'I discovered I had to be careful − to use the information the emotions conveyed to me but not let the messenger make the decisions.'

'I still don't understand exactly what you mean,' said Hasan, though he was beginning to become more relaxed in her presence. Quickly he forgot her disability as well as how briefly he had known her. He was in her confidence as though they had been eternal friends.

'Let me see,' she said, looking out into the garden trees as she struggled for a way to make her thoughts clear. 'Do you think guilt is good or bad?'

'It's bad,' said Hasan. 'It makes me feel bad, so bad I sometimes can't even pray.'

'But it isn't the guilt, you see? The guilt is a message from yourself to yourself. Your emotions are telling you there is a conflict some-where. Your feelings are letting you know that your actions are not measuring up to your expectations you have for yourself.'

'What should I do, then?'

'Simple. Get rid of the conflict. Either change your goals, or else change your actions.'

'You make it sound so simple,' said Hasan.

'It's not a one-time thing,' said Rezvani, leaning back and clasping her hands together in her lap. 'As Bahá'u'lláh says, we must bring ourselves to account each day − we must evaluate how we have acted in terms of what we expect from ourselves as Bahá'ís.'

'In other words, you think guilt is a good thing?'

'Guilt, healthy guilt, is a constant companion of anyone who wants to go beyond where they are, at least a certain amount of it.'

'Why?'

'Because if you wish to strive to do better, you have to set your goals higher than where you are, right?'

'True.'

'Which means that you are going to feel some sort of tension.'

'But what do you mean by "healthy" guilt. How can guilt be "unhealthy" if it is simply a messenger?'

She paused again, then looked at her legs, motionless beneath the long dress and strapped to the chair beneath the folds of cloth. 'Sometimes after a long day,' she said, placing both palms on her knees, 'I feel my legs move. They don't really move, of course. They never will, not of their own power. Yet occasionally the feeling is there, as real as it ever was before the accident. You see, there's nothing wrong with the muscles or the bones – only the nerves, the messengers are damaged. Usually they send no messages at all – that's the problem; but sometimes I have the sensation of movement – the nerves send false messages to my brain.

'Emotions can be the same,' she continued. 'Some people may feel immense guilt for no good reason simply because their emotions are ill. But there is an even more insidious way that emotions can become disturbed. In many countries people take opium and other narcotics to deceive their emotions, to tell the brain they feel wonderful when there is no reason to feel that way.'

'To send false messages.'

'Exactly.'

'That's what alcohol does,' said Hasan.

'Do you understand what I mean, then? Some people live for their emotions. Instead of doing things that satisfy their noble goals, they play tricks on themselves, make the emotions send false messages, or else they live only for the emotion itself. Instead of living up to their expectations and then feeling good about themselves, they do only what feels good.'

'But what is wrong with that?' asked Hasan. 'As long as the feelings are based on something real?'

'Because what we feel in the beginning of learning something or striving to accomplish something is not always a good indication of what we will feel later on. Let me give you an example. When all of these things happened to Father and me, we felt as though we would never recover, never be happy again, or even sane. And yet here we are, stronger and better for what we have endured.'

Hasan looked at her again, the deeply beautiful eyes, the strength in that expression. There was no way she could be feigning such valour, he thought, and for whom would she put on such an act? Her courage was real, her wisdom gained from sorrow and struggle, the only trustworthy wisdom there was.

'Hasan,' she said, after a long pause, 'do you truly believe your parents are well-off in the spiritual realm?'

'Yes,' he admitted, for the first time. 'Sometimes I even feel them with me, as if they see what I do and give me help.'

'And do you believe that there is really nothing you can do to see that justice is done?'

'I suppose not,' said Hasan, realizing with clarity that neither he nor anyone else had the power to rectify the situation, not now.

'Then leave the perpetrators to God! After all, He is a sufficient judge. You will never know what was in their hearts. Simply pray that they learn from what they did and pray that you will never do anything similar.'

She pushed her chair forward so she was directly in front of him. She reached out and took his hand as a nurse might take the hand of a small child.

'When Bahá'u'lláh was being taken to the Síyáh-Chál as a prisoner, He was berated at every step by the crowd of people who had come to insult Him. He marched barefooted and bareheaded in the hot sun. They threw rocks. They reviled Him with crude names. But as He walked, an aged woman broke from the crowd. She held a stone in her hand and cried out, "Give me a chance to fling my stone in his face!" Bahá'u'lláh stopped and asked the guards to permit her to throw the stone, saying, "Deny her not what she regards as a meritorious act in the sight of God."'

'I don't understand what you are implying,' Hasan admitted.

'My point is that eventually you must realize that the malice you bear those nameless, faceless people does not affect them in any way, nor does it soothe your parents who pray only for their son's advancement in the kingdoms of God.'

She released his hand, but continued to look at his face until he pulled his head up and looked back. He said nothing. He raised his eyes, and the gloomy aspect had vanished slightly and he smiled. Her reasoning was simple, clear and undeniable. He repeated the thought several times to himself, then said, 'I wish to go to the Qiblih now.' The tone of his voice made her rejoice inside. 'Will you be here tomorrow?' he asked.

'Do you wish me to be?' she asked.

'Yes, I do,' said Hasan. 'But tell me something before I go.'

'What is that?'

'Why is it that you are so young and yet you know so much about the Tablets of Bahá'u'lláh?'

'For a year there was little else to do but read.'

'I will say prayers for you,' he said as he got up to depart.

'And I for you,' she said as she waved goodbye.

16

The New Jerusalem

HASAN left the Riḍván Gardens and walked to the Mansion of Bahjí so wrapped in thought that he was barely aware of his own footsteps. Over and over in his mind he recalled the expression on Rezvani's face as she had talked about her mother's death, how she had managed to deal with her confused feelings about those horrible events. This was no textbook advice, no casual aphorism. Hers was insight achieved through the pain of experience.

As he neared the Qiblih, he was tempted to berate himself — how could he, a healthy young man, be so overwhelmed by his emotions ten years after the fact, while Rezvani with all the more reason to grieve was triumphant, strong, detached. Then he remembered what she had said about emotions, those subtle messengers. No, the conflict he felt was real. It may have been set aside for ten years, delayed until he had the wherewithal to face this inner struggle, but he had no reason to feel guilty about his sense of loss.

When at last he found himself alone in the garden room that sheltered the entrance to the small square building where lay entombed the earthly remains of Bahá'u'lláh, Hasan's prayers were effortless and powerful. As he prayed, he forced himself to imagine the villagers in Yazd who had been responsible for his parents' deaths, not as in his dreams, masks of faceless evil. Now he could envision

faces, real people, perhaps people he had known, whose shops he had
entered, whose goods his parents had purchased. Perhaps they
thought of themselves as fine citizens, as dutiful Muslims, or
possibly, just possibly, like him, they dreamed. Perhaps some nights
alone with their thoughts they struggled with the ignominy of their
wretched choices.

He could not know their motives, their hearts, the circumstances
that might have led them to his home that night. He could imagine
that some believed themselves to be doing the *right* thing. He could
not forgive them that − it was not his place to do so − but he could
follow Rezvani's example. He could let go.

That was the key, to let go, to accept in his heart as he had in his
head that there was nothing more for him to do to rectify the crime.

He said another prayer. Something even more profound came to
him, the notion that he could not have done anything to prevent it. He
realized that in his most secret heart he had long harboured guilt
about that night, a feeling that he should not have slept, that at the
very least he could have been awake to bid them farewell.

Rezvani's story echoed in his mind, especially her description of
lying helpless, watching the house go up in flames with her mother
inside. Sometimes there was nothing to do about the tragedies of life,
nothing to do but endure them, to learn from them, and in time to
accept them. Sometimes justice had to be left to God alone.

He thought about what he had learned over the past months about
the effect of his parents' martyrdom on the Bahá'í community, how
their sacrifice had energized the hearts of others. Now Hasan was
beginning to realize that he personally could serve their memory more
profoundly by devoting himself in service to the principles for which
they had stood firm. That was the answer, then − not to forget them,
not war against remembrance, but neither to harbour guilt or vengeance, rather to translate their courage and faith into actions. After
all, 'Abdu'l-Bahá Himself had mentioned that the prayers for those
in the next world as well as acts done in their name would assist them
in their eternal progress.

It would take time. For so many years he had unknowingly held tenaciously to a sense of familial obligation to avenge their deaths. Relinquishing all those feelings would not happen magically. 'But that's the way anything valuable happens,' he thought, remembering Moayyed's observation about the swimmers.

And there was time, after all. There was time and there was a way, the Bahá'í way. Suddenly that thought struck him as remarkable. 'I am a Bahá'í!' he whispered. 'I have chosen this!' Everything had happened so quickly he had never really had an occasion to contemplate this profound change in his life. Here he was at the Shrine of Bahá'u'lláh, a place sacred to his new-found beliefs. The thought filled him with pride, with strength, with a sense of belonging and inner peace he had never before felt, and softly he recited the new name he bore like a badge of honour.

The next morning Hasan dressed and ate eagerly. He had said nothing to his aunt or uncle, not even to Ali, about his talk with Rezvani. He was not sure why. By ten o'clock he had already walked the distance to the garden and sat impatiently on the bench waiting for Rezvani to appear. At every rustling of leaves he would look down the garden path.

He marvelled at his own impatience. What exactly did he expect? What could she say that Moayyed or Ali or other Bahá'ís had not already told him?

He had no answer, yet he was filled with anticipation of her visit. A few minutes later he heard the far-off rattle of carriage wheels on the rocky path that led to the arch over the garden entrance. Hasan stood up. He could barely see the carriage through the thick foliage, but there she was, seated beside a powerfully-built driver whom Hasan presumed to be her father.

The man had a stern, regal face, the sort one might expect of a military officer or high official. He pulled the carriage to a halt, dismounted and went around to the back where he unstrapped the wheelchair and placed it on the ground. Then he came around to the other side and in one sweeping motion he picked up his daughter as if she were utterly weightless. He placed her in the chair with such gentleness, such respect that Hasan's eyes suddenly moistened, so touched was he by the sight of this wordless affection between father and daughter.

With deft strength she crossed the bridge into the garden. 'Did you think I wasn't coming?' she asked merrily as she manoeuvred the wheelchair in front of the bench.

'I hoped you would,' said Hasan. He proceeded to tell her about his visit to the Shrine of Bahá'u'lláh. He told her how much better he felt as a result of their conversation.

She smiled. 'It is amazing, isn't it? Words, conversations, ideas — they have no shape, no weight or size or colour, but they have more power than all the combined machines mankind has invented.'

Rezvani and Hasan did not stay long. They talked little of the serious matters of the previous day, but instead Rezvani took Hasan on a tour of the garden, introduced him to the variety of plants as if they were her family or close friends. Then they sat and tried to spot a songbird whose melody filled the morning air.

'It always seems so sane and peaceful here,' she said. 'I suspect that's why Bahá'u'lláh called this place His New Jerusalem. Here and at the Shrine of the Báb I feel I can almost glimpse the possibilities of the future.'

'I have never been to the Shrine of the Báb,' said Hasan.

'No? Oh, you must go!' said Rezvani emphatically. 'I would love to take you there. I tell you what, tomorrow Father and I are going there to say prayers for Mother. Many Bahá'ís go to Haifa for prayers at the Shrine. Let me go ask Father right now.'

'But your father doesn't know who I am.'

'Of course he does. I told him all about you.'

His daughter's request touched the heart of Reza Tawfiq Bushrú'í. The face which seemed to have an implacable expression broke into a most delightful grin, and his soft voice assented.

'A fine idea,' he said. 'Just what we all need on these hot summer days.'

Hasan hurried home to tell Aunt Nahid about his proposed trip to

Mt Carmel. 'It's only a short way,' he said before she had a chance to answer.

'Just a minute,' she said. 'First, where did you meet Rezvani?'

'I was at the Riḍván Gardens yesterday and she was there too.'

'By herself?'

'No, with her father.'

'Yes, I believe I know her. She arrived this year from Búshihr. I believe she is crippled, isn't she?'

'What? Oh, yes.'

'Well, I was hoping that we would be the first to take you,' said Nahid, but when she saw the disappointment on his face, she added quickly, 'but perhaps we can go another time.' She paused. 'I know ! We will also go tomorrow! After all, we are one family here.' She hugged Hasan, delighting in the apparent healing of his spirit. She stepped back and looked at him, his broad shoulders and head erect, the deep colour of his sunburned cheeks. He looked so grown up in his taj and waistcoat, and his eyes seemed so clear and contented. 'Can this be the same Hasan that appeared at our door?'

'No,' said Hasan. 'It is not the same Hasan.'

The next morning Ali and Hasan dressed together. Both were excited about the day's journey to Mt Carmel. Ali listened with interest to Hasan tell of the chance meeting in the garden. He tried to follow Hasan's breathless summary of the discussion, but it was impossible. His cousin's enthusiasm muddled whatever thread of logic might have made sense of the reportage. But Ali smiled and nodded – he understood the heart of the matter, that Hasan was at peace with himself.

Precisely at eight o'clock the make-shift carriage pulled up with Rezvani's father looking stern as ever and Rezvani herself strapped in the carriage seat that her father had designed especially for her. Hasan introduced Rezvani and her father to Ali and to Uncle Husayn and Aunt Nahid.

After cordial greetings, Hasan climbed into the back seat, and the carriage made its way along the stone streets of 'Akká, its wheels

echoing from the old buildings that lined the way. It was a good time
of day, the merchants readying their shops, the streets just beginning
to fill up with busy townspeople. Reza held the reins loosely, con-
fidently guiding the horse through the land gate and onto the road
that linked Haifa and 'Akká.'

Reza kept the carriage to the side of the road to make room for the
occasional car that would pass by noisily, scaring horses and evoking
snarls from the slow-moving pedestrians and merchants leading their
donkeys.

'It is all changing so quickly,' said Rezvani. 'Some day this road
will be filled with people making their way to the Shrine of the Báb.'

'Some day people will look to the Shrine of the Báb and the gardens
as an emblem of the Bay of Haifa,' said Reza, proud of his own work
there. 'Some day this place will be more important than Jerusalem
itself as a symbol of God's Covenant – of course, not during my
lifetime.'

'Don't be such a pessimist, Father. You know as well as I that
history is not changed by masses of people, but by a few dedicated
souls.'

Hasan watched the father and daughter, studied their gestures,
their expressions. He sensed that Rezvani was more resolved than her
father about the death of her mother, more resilient, perhaps because
she had been forced to deal with her own wounds and feelings.
Perhaps in coming to terms with the finality of her physical loss she
had also come to accept the finality of her earthly separation from her
mother. What was more, it had to weigh heavily on Reza that he had
been away from home when the terror had struck. What Hasan
sensed was that Reza had to endure the daily pain of seeing his beautiful and once active daughter confined to her wheelchair. Not a day
went by that he did not look at her face and recall a small giggling
child dancing in the hallway. Not a day passed that he was not
shocked to see her so changed.

And yet her spirit was dauntless as ever, stronger perhaps. Reza
would watch his daughter pore over the writings of the Báb, of
Bahá'u'lláh and 'Abdu'l-Bahá. Sometimes after he had gone to bed,

he would hear her chanting prayers on into the morning. And though he helped her throughout the day, with the assistance of an old woman who was wonderfully kind, he knew in his heart that she was the stronger one, she was the comforter.

None of this was ever said, that the strong merchant of Búshihr who lifted his daughter like a leaf looked to her for strength. It did not need to be spoken − both knew it was so and, if the truth were known, neither minded.

'Do you know how the Shrine came to be built?' Reza asked Hasan.

'Ali told me that Bahá'u'lláh directed 'Abdu'l-Bahá to build it.'

Reza snapped the reins ever so gently. 'Yes, and do you know how the remains of the Báb were brought here?'

'No,' said Hasan.

'It's quite a story. After the Báb was executed in Tabríz with His young follower Anís, their bodies were left beside a moat, guarded so that they could not receive a proper burial.'

'Why was that?' asked Hasan.

'There is a Muslim tradition which says that the body of the Promised Imam will be preserved from beasts of prey. The officials were thinking that if the bodies were left exposed, it was likely the remains would be carried off by wild dogs and the people could no longer contend that the Báb fulfilled the prophecies of Islam.

'The next night a Bábí named Ḥájí Sulaymán Khán had the bodies removed to a silk factory owned by one of the believers. There they were placed in a wooden casket. When the bodies disappeared, the mullas presumed the corpses had been devoured by wild animals. They boasted that the Báb could not possibly have been the Imam because the tradition had been violated.

'For years the remains were transferred from one hiding place to another, first to Ṭihrán. Finally, when 'Abdu'l-Bahá was ready, they were sent here in 1899 where for ten years they were kept hidden in the room of the Greatest Holy Leaf in the House of 'Abdu'lláh Páshá in 'Akká. Then in 1909, after the building and vault were completed on Mt Carmel, 'Abdu'l-Bahá had the marble sarcophagus moved to the vault.'

'Then it actually took fifty-nine years?' asked Hasan.

'Yes,' said Rezvani. 'When the casket was finally in place in the sarcophagus, 'Abdu'l-Bahá was so overcome with joy that he took off His turban and shoes, placed His forehead on the open casket, and began to weep so loudly that everyone else there wept as well.'

'That's hard for me to imagine,' said Hasan, ''Abdu'l-Bahá weeping. When I saw Him, it seemed that no power on earth could touch Him.'

'Perhaps no power on earth could constrain Him,' Reza commented, 'but never believe that 'Abdu'l-Bahá is unaffected by the human condition. He takes to heart all human misery.'

The three continued to talk as the wagon made a hypnotic sort of creaking along the road, Hasan soon discovered that Rezvani's father was not at all as he had thought. Far from being reserved or stern, he was quite open with his thoughts and feelings. He seemed to be completely comfortable talking to this young man whom he had only just met. Perhaps it was his awareness of Hasan's loss, the sense of shared grief, that enabled him to open up to Hasan.

When they reached the base of the mountain, Reza tied the carriage and took his daughter in his arms. He had walked only a few paces when three or four Bahá'í men, also on their way up the mountain, offered assistance.

'Please, sir,' said a young voice from behind, 'let *me* help!'

Reza turned to see a young village boy. He was not a Bahá'í and not very well off. He had a small, two-wheeled cart pulled by a rather large goat.

'Do you know where we are going?' asked Hasan.

'To the Holy Shrine of Master 'Abbás,' said the boy, who, like most of the poor in 'Akká and Haifa, regarded 'Abdu'l-Bahá as their personal friend and foster-father. In fact, they called Him 'Father of the Poor' because He would regularly distribute alms to the needy with His own hands.

'Please,' insisted the young boy again, 'it would be to my honour.' Reza looked at his daughter. With a smile she assented, and her father placed her gently in the cart, which had plenty of room for her to sit comfortably facing the rear. The tilt of the small vehicle offered a secure angle for her along the steep track up to the Shrine. Hasan walked behind. He could not help marvelling at how the young woman could manage such dignity and bearing in that strange little cart.

There were a few other believers at the Tomb itself, the men waiting patiently at one door, the women at another, so that all could have a chance to sit quietly in the peacefulness of the Shrine and pray. Hasan was excited but somewhat anxious as he waited with Rezvani's father outside the door to the chamber.

Rezvani sat with the women on the other side of the Tomb on a small chair her father had carried up the mountain, a folding wooden chair he always carried in the back of the carriage for such occasions. The little boy with the goat cart had left, smiling, radiant from his good deed and refusing all efforts to compensate him for his kindness.

Finally it was the turn of Ali and Rezvani's father to enter the Shrine. They removed their shoes, and moved with dignity and reverence into the vaulted chamber.

As soon as Hasan entered, he was overwhelmed by the sanctity of the simple stone structure, the stuccoed walls, the floor covered with a magnificent Persian carpet of intricate design. From the outside it had seemed an ordinary rectangular stone edifice with two sets of doors at the southwest end. But when he entered, Hasan saw that it was not just one room and then another. In line with the outside door was a threshold to an inner room in the centre of the building. On the floor of the inner room were exquisite glass vases with candles burning in them. They were set in groups of three and glowed in that room like flowers of living flame.

The doorway into the inner Shrine was arched, and beneath it was a raised threshold on which had been placed fresh rose petals from the garden. As they entered, a caretaker at the entrance anointed their hands with rose water as a token of joy. Rezvani's father went immediately to the threshold where he touched his forehead to the green cloth then prostrated himself in prayer.

Hasan was startled by what he felt in this place. He slowly seated himself where he was, near the back of the room. From there he could see the inner chamber where the sarcophagus lay entombed. Before him and around him were one or two other Bahá'ís in various attitudes of devotion.

He had been to holy places before, but this was something quite different − the unassuming reverence of humble believers in this inconspicuous and simple place of adoration. Soon Hasan was lost in his own thoughts and feelings and he became oblivious to those around him. His eyes focused on the beauty of that inner room bathed in light. He thought of Anís, the youth buried in this place of honour with his Beloved Báb, this young man who had earned a place of eternal glory. And why? Because at a crucial moment of choice he had obeyed his Lord.

How many prayers had now been said in the youth's honour because of one noble response? How many more would in ages to come urge him along on his eternal journey? 'Oh, give me grace to do some noble deed,' prayed Hasan in a whisper.

Suddenly tears welled up in his eyes. He did not know why; he only knew they would not cease. He remained outwardly calm and silent, but the tears streamed down his cheeks, and a great lump in his throat made him want to sob out loud, but he restrained himself. He became unaware of the chamber and everyone in it as the candle lights refracted through his tears like fountains of sparkling fire. Feelings flowed through his veins in a torrent, almost terrifying him, except . . . except that it felt good somehow, this purging, this cleansing, as if venom was being drained from the deep recesses of an ancient wound.

Suddenly, he was overwhelmed by the sensation that he had been to this spot before, or at least that he had felt these things before, this ecstasy. It was like a distant bell tolling, or a faintly remembered melody. Yes, that was it − like the song his mother sang − gentle and lovely, humming a lullaby. Then he remembered eyes, dark and endless eyes, and a fragrance of roses.

In his mind's eye he began to see the hazy outline of a garden, a small rose garden outside a bedroom window. He could see it clearly now. His father was out there — his father was always there hoeing in the sun, turning dry desert soil in a rhythm, and the sound of his hoe so like the crunching of roasted sunflower seeds. Then he recalled something more — his father reaching down to kiss him. He could feel heat radiating from the sunburned face. He felt his father reach down to touch rose-scented fingers to Hasan's neck and cheeks. He could feel his father's soft beard against his face. He could make out the shape of the eyes, wrinkled at the corners, and always smiling, always smiling.

So many images flashed through Hasan's mind, each one quickly fading into another, each one so long forgotten and yet now recalled with perfect clarity, fresh as yesterday and palpable to his senses. How long had they dwelled in the storehouse of his memory, withheld from his conscious mind until, until . . . until what? Until he was ready?

Hasan lowered his head into his hands. He felt the tear flood subside, like a cask of vintage wine finally emptied to the lees. He was calm. The room was clear. The light in the inner chamber flickered and the low murmur of chanted prayers filled the room.

The memories still hovered in Hasan's mind, those images from so long ago. But they were his now. He had mastery over them. They were his to keep, like precious mementoes he could bring out whenever he wished to recall his cherished heritage. Yes, he could visit his past with impunity, could smell his father's prize blossoms, eat his mother's delicate pastries, feel again his parents' tender affection. He could even hum the bedtime tune his mother sang. Even that was his again.

Later Hasan sat outside the Shrine with Rezvani and her father. Ali, Aunt Nahid, Uncle Husayn and Moayyed had arrived and offered prayers at the Shrine. Now they all sat together quietly, and Hasan looked out across the bright blue water of the bay at the city of 'Akká in the distance — ancient 'Akká, the holy city gleaming white in the noon sun. Like him, the city seemed to be recovering its lost spirit.

The other Bahá'ís had walked up to the promontory of the

mountain, the site where Bahá'u'lláh had revealed the Tablet of Carmel. But the path was too rough for Rezvani, so this gathering decided to sit among the flowers in the small garden surrounding the Tomb of the Báb.

Hasan told no one what had occurred in the Shrine, but Nahid commented, 'You seem most content today, Hasan.' He was still so lost in thought that he could say nothing in response, though he could not suppress the huge smile that suddenly brushed across his face.

'Already it is so different here!' said Husayn to the others, trying to change the subject so that Hasan would not feel embarrassed. 'When Nahid and I came here over ten years ago this was all barren. There was no Tomb, no buildings or trees whatsoever on this mountain, except for the monastery. So infertile a place you have never seen, almost solid rock and no water to speak of. Who among us would have believed that even the Master could change it into a garden?'

'It is only just beginning,' said Reza knowledgeably, privileged as he felt to be working as a gardener for the Master. 'Some day this will all be magnificent — terraces of flowers and trees, a great stairway from the Shrine down to the village below!'

Rezvani agreed. 'In the Tablet of Carmel Bahá'u'lláh says: "Call out to Zion, O Carmel, and announce the joyful tidings; He that was hidden from mortal eyes is come!" Then towards the end He says: "Ere long will God sail His Ark upon thee, and will manifest the people of Bahá who have been mentioned in the Book of Names."'

'As this Faith spreads and grows and enlightens the planet,' added Moayyed, 'so this mountainside will become a spiritual refuge and a source of divine authority for the whole of mankind, not for the Bahá'ís only.'

Usually Moayyed spoke humbly, in mild tones, but now his voice resounded with authority. And each of them listened with respect because in some way they were all his children.

After Moayyed had explained some of what he understood about the future of Mt Carmel, the gathering of family and friends stayed to eat a light repast. Hasan wandered off by himself a short distance from the others. Moayyed found him beside the pathway sitting on a large boulder.

Hasan remarked how beautiful it was to look out over the bay, to survey the places that now meant so much to him. Then he turned to Moayyed. 'Will it all happen as you say? Will there really come a day when this mountain will be a garden and Bahá'ís will meet together to make decisions about the destiny of the whole world?'

'My son,' said Moayyed, 'it will happen in your own lifetime!'

Hasan looked at the grim certitude on that wondrous countenance and he knew it would be so. He then looked back to 'Akká. 'Sir, what happens now?'

Moayyed broke into a most heartfelt smile. He sensed that something profound had happened in Hasan, and he felt an inner delight that he might have played a part in the process of that transformation. 'What happens now? Well, I will tell you. It was not enough that Bahá'u'lláh told us who we are or what we are. No, He also brought us a plan of action, a way − laws to safeguard us, institutions to guide us so that we might give physical form to this spiritual vision.'

'The New Jerusalem?' asked Hasan.

'Exactly! God's kingdom come to earth, but built one stone at a time. To know and to worship, you see? They are inseparable − the knowledge and the deed together. Now that you know, you have only half the task completed. You must do something with the knowledge you have gained. You must change something.'

Neither spoke for a while as they continued to view the endless beauty of the perspective from atop Carmel.

'Will I always feel this good?' asked Hasan after awhile.

'No,' said Moayyed. 'At times you may feel sorrow, even despair, but there will also be times, my fine young friend, when you will feel even better than now.'

'Sir, I feel as if I have come on a long, long journey. I feel I have come such a great distance that I can't remember what I used to feel even weeks ago.'

Moayyed looked at the much-changed young man and recited a

verse from Rúmí: 'When we finally achieve the goal of our journey and the end of our search, we forget all that has happened along the way.'

Hasan was silent for a moment, then asked, 'Will I ever again be as I was?'

'A rose cannot become the bud. A mighty oak cannot become an acorn. And who would wish it otherwise?'

'Not I,' said Hasan. 'Certainly not I.'